How to Get Grant Money in the Humanities and Social Sciences

T0373198

How to Get Grant Money in the Humanities and Social Sciences

RAPHAEL B. FOLSOM

Yale UNIVERSITY PRESS/NEW HAVEN & LONDON

Published with assistance from the Louis Stern Memorial Fund.

Yale University Press books may be purchased in quantity for educational, business, or promotional use. For information, please e-mail sales.press@yale.edu (U.S. office) or sales@yaleup.co.uk (U.K. office).

Designed by Mary Valencia.
Set in Joanna MT type by IDS Infotech, Ltd.
Printed in the United States of America.

Library of Congress Control Number: 2018901962
ISBN 978-0-300-21743-8 (paperback : alk. paper)

A catalogue record for this book is available from the British Library.

This paper meets the requirements of ANSI/NISO Z39.48–1992 (Permanence of Paper).

10 9 8 7 6 5 4 3 2 1

For Sandra

[The evaluation of grant proposals is] just very pragmatic. You put twelve pretty smart people in a windowless room in [some city] for two days and you expect them to remain sane. They're pretty professional people, so they do their best. They have very different tastes so there's a lot of potential for conflict. They stay cool-headed and they have to make these heroic efforts to agree across big disciplinary differences on what constitutes a good proposal . . . we spend so much time on it and . . . there's so many people focusing at once on this proposal. . . . This year particularly, there was a lot of movement: You had a lot of situations where something was ranked relatively high [prior to the meeting and] weaknesses were discussed and people in favor were convinced [not to fund]. And conversely, something [ranked] quite low, [but] the more you talked about it, the more it looked like you should give it a chance, that it had some promise. . . . It would be sort of self-congratulatory to say that cream rises to the top and that we picked exactly the right set. I don't think that happened. But I think we chose on average the better proposals.

—An economist interviewed by Michèle Lamont on reviewing grant proposals, quoted in How Professors Think, Inside the Curious World of Academic Judgment (2010)

Contents

Acknowledgments

All scholarship, all books, all articles—indeed life itself—are team efforts. No amount of thanks is enough for the help and encouragement I've received over the years. A few teammates deserve special notice. Gilbert Joseph, adviser, mentor, and friend, led the dissertation prospectus workshop I took in grad school, which I later reconfigured as a workshop on grant writing for graduate students at the University of Oklahoma. Like many books, this one is the fruit of a seed Gil planted many years ago. My wife, Sandra Folsom, had the idea that I should turn my grant workshop into a book. That is only one of the countless reasons this book would not exist without her. My old boss, John Isaacson, taught me most of what I know about institutions, and showed me the value of being a giver. Colleagues at the University of Oklahoma read parts of the manuscript and offered crucial advice: many thanks to Ronnie Grinberg, Erika Robb Larkins, Kim Marshall, and Andreana Prichard. My excellent first editor, Laura Davulis, asked me to send her a proposal for the book and eventually signed it before moving on to new challenges. And my current editor, Jaya Chatterjee, has seen it through to completion with wit, warmth, and patience. Special thanks to the nine eminent scholars who agreed to be interviewed for this project. The University of Oklahoma and the American Council of Learned Societies provided funding crucial to this project. A thousand thanks to you all.

INTRODUCTION

For a variety of reasons, including merit, hard work, good luck, and the generous patronage of powerful people in my field, I have received a variety of substantial grants to support my research. Here is a partial list of those I've won:

- The Mellon Fellowship in the Humanities.
- A Mellon grant for Latin American history at Yale.
- The Fox Fellowship for a year's study at El Colégio de México.
- The Fulbright-Hays International Dissertation Research Fellowship.
- The Clements Center Postdoctoral Fellowship.
- The Santander Visiting Fellowship at the David Rockefeller Center for Latin American Studies, Harvard.
- The Charles A. Ryskamp Research Fellowship of the American Council of Learned Societies.

I suspect that a great yet unjust principle of American life—Money Attracts Money—has also been at work here. Every grant opens doors to more grants, leading to a circumstance in which it seems that those who least need funding receive the most of it. Is this unfair? Possibly. There are arguments to be made on both sides of the question. But one thing is clear: research funding is not distributed evenly across the profession. Some people get much more of it than others do, and that funding places them at a distinct advantage. If the research funding system is indeed unfair, it is also clear that, when it is unfair in your favor, it can make life quite pleasant.

In this book, I describe what has worked for me in the past, and what I think may work for you as you seek funding in the social sciences and humanities. My intended readers are precocious undergrads interested in scholarships for graduate school, graduate students who are trying to secure research funding and postdoctoral fellowships, and younger faculty members attempting to fund new projects and move up in the profession.

Grants are important first and foremost because they give you time away from teaching, and money to live on, while doing research. But the process of applying for grants is important too, because it focuses your mind on a harsh yet beautiful fact of academic life: whatever you write about, you are writing for a market. Some markets are as broad as the reading public of the United States. Other markets are as narrow as a dozen specialists working in a small field. But whatever market you are writing for, you should never forget what it is. Markets mean competition, and market competition produces stark outcomes ranging from dazzling opportunity to, much more often, the anguish of defeat. In order to succeed in your market of choice, you must shine. You must offer something that people are willing to pay for. You must refine your thinking more fully, perhaps, than you ever expected you would or could. There are deep satisfactions to the work of refining your scholarship in this way, whether your project gets funding or not. Beyond the money, those deep intellectual satisfactions are why I think the process of grant writing is worthwhile.

Which brings us to my brief description of the principles and processes of getting research money. Three general principles to keep in mind:

1. Competition is a fact of academic life. For as long as you are an academic researcher, you will be asking people for money. Practice and guidance in the craft of grant writing will give you a leg up on the competition. And make no mistake: academia is competitive, and the competition never ends.

2. Ambition is a useful tool. By aiming for the stars, you may or may not hit them. But if you don't hit the stars, you could very well hit the treetops. By aiming only for the treetops, you may well hit the ground. Aiming low usually means striking lower. Never count yourself out of the tougher competitions before you enter them.

3. You need a team. This team should include mentors who know your work and support it, and equally important, peers whom you like and trust, and who can give you constructive feedback on your work.

Every successful grant application has six parts:

1. A research question. You need a research question that can be stated in a single sentence.

2. Subject matter. You need to identify what historians call primary sources with great specificity, such that the granting institution knows you will hit the ground running once you get to the site (or sites) of your research.

3. Scholarship. You must master the scholarly literature bearing on your topic.

4. Theory. You must show how your work is informed by a body of humanistic or social scientific theory.

5. Funding sources. You need to find out who has money to distribute.

6. Criteria. You have to know in great detail what each of the grant-making institutions you are contacting is looking for.

Here are four steps to producing a winning grant proposal. I recommend that you commit to completing one step per month, and that you do these steps with a writing group. This group can include as few as two people or as many as fifteen. More than that and things become unwieldy.

1. Before your first meeting, read this book, draft a research question, make a list of sources you want to examine, create a list of ten grants you want to apply for, and send emails to three possible recommenders asking them for a letter, to be delivered in four months. Then get together with your group for an informal conversation about all of this.

2. For your second meeting, bring a rough outline of your proposal and a select bibliography. The outline should take the form of a one-page, single-spaced list of ideas and facts that you want to include in the final product. The bibliography should be no more than two single-spaced pages.
3. For your third meeting, you should bring a complete draft of the proposal, which others in the seminar will read and critique.
4. For your fourth meeting, invite two or three outsiders to read all the final proposals, evaluate them, rank them from best to worst, and, as needed, explain their rankings.

That's it! It sounds simple and easy, but in fact the process is complex and difficult. The rest of the book will walk you through it, with each part illuminating one piece of the research funding puzzle. Part 1 provides a brief guide to my general principles of grant writing. Part 2 includes a detailed description of the ingredients of a successful grant proposal. Part 3 is a syllabus of sorts, providing a step-by-step guide for a group of grant writers as they move from first glimmerings to finished product. And Part 4 offers insights from top scholars in various fields with broad experience in the writing and evaluation of grant and fellowship proposals.

Can a book like this one be useful to people working in multiple disciplines? The humorist Robert Benchley once mused that there are two kinds of people: people who say there are two kinds of people, and people who don't. To put it another way, some professors think that the disciplines are unique and deeply peculiar, and that knowledge and methods from one discipline are rarely applicable in another; others think that the disciplines can and should be in constant dialogue and that scholars in various disciplines are eminently capable of educating, and learning from, one another. I fall in the latter group—in part because I work in the discipline of history, which is the magpie of the departments, and tends to decorate its nest with methods and ideas from all over campus. I also take the latter position for a practical reason, and I think you should too. The evaluators of grant applications very often read material from outside the fields they were trained in. If you are an art historian and the reader of your application is an economist, it behooves you write in such a way that your contribution is comprehensible to her. That is why it is possible, and indeed desirable, for a book like this to address grant writers in multiple disciplines. It is essential that grant applications have elements that are appealing *across* disciplines. What I attempt to do here, then, is to use examples from literary studies, art history, political science, anthropology, and history in order to define certain broad measures of quality that apply to most disciplines in the humanities and social sciences most of the time.

Part I

PRINCIPLES

Chapter 1

PREPARE FOR A COMPETITIVE PROCESS

I recently made a fascinating discovery in one of the most ill-organized archives I've ever had the displeasure of working in: my own file cabinet. I had long wanted to purge my files, and finally, when there were too many papers in my office for me to get anything done at all, I made time to do it. In the process, I found a folder from 2011 containing a rejection letter from the American Council of Learned Societies (ACLS). It thanked me for my application for the Charles A. Ryskamp Research Fellowship, and said that of 194 applications, only ten were selected.

I was floored, for a couple of reasons. I was amazed at my own stupidity in applying for a grant that I was not eligible for (it is for people who are further along in their careers than I was at the time). I was also very surprised that I did not have the foggiest memory of having applied for it. When I did in fact receive the Ryskamp three years later, I was sure that I had gotten it on my first try. This would have made it the exception among all the grants I've gotten in my career. It has usually taken me two or three tries to receive any grant or fellowship. But no, the Ryskamp was not the exception. I had applied for it, and had been rejected, once before.

I was sad that I didn't nail the Ryskamp on my first attempt, but I was happy to find proof that I had practiced something I preach: I had focused on the application rather than the outcome. I always tell graduate students that you can measure your progress in academia by the number of rejection letters you get. Getting rejected for grants, fellowships, jobs, and publications of all kinds means you are putting your ideas out there. You are testing them against tough competition, learning from that competition, and soldiering on. My little discovery revealed that by 2011, I had become so inured to rejection that the letter from the ACLS had not just failed to deter me from applying again—it had failed to cause even the slightest ripple in my consciousness. I had filed the rejection letter and forgotten all about it.

For people who are applying for grants for the first time, the competitiveness of the enterprise can be dispiriting. Human beings have a natural tendency to extrapolate into the future from limited experience. For instance, a thirteen-year-old might think, "I asked my first love to the junior high school prom and she said no. No one will ever love me. I'm a loser. I might as well give up on love and become a hermit." Though they are often more than twenty years older than that junior-high-school reject, many grant applicants persist in thinking along the same lines, and take individual rejections as an indication that their work lacks value. It usually isn't true.

I am here to tell you that if you keep working hard, keep thinking, keep learning, and keep applying and applying and applying, you will receive funding for your research. There is a novelist named Curtis Sittenfeld who wrote a novel called Cipher that no fewer than twenty publishers rejected. The final one said yes, gave Sittenfeld a $40,000 advance, and changed the title of the novel from Cipher to Prep. Prep sold 133,000 copies in hardcover, and, at last count, 339,000 copies in paperback. Prep has been translated into twenty-five languages and continues to sell. If, like Curtis Sittenfeld, you are willing to work hard and brave rejection over and over again, good things will happen.[1]

None of this is to imply that the competition is pleasant or easy. It is not, and nothing can make it so. When I was in graduate school, several of the most revered professors in my department received wildly negative reviews of their work in the scholarly press. One professor published an edited volume that a reviewer described as a "joke." The celebrated anthropologist Claude Lévi-Strauss emerged from retirement (or was it the grave?) to accuse one of my teachers of being a Holocaust denier. (He is not one.) Another professor had his book described as "caricatured" and "doing more harm than good." And one especially unhinged critic thought a book by one of my teachers was so bad that he cordially invited the author to commit suicide. (That book went on to win the National Book Award.) Mind you, all the recipients of these reviews hold endowed chairs at Yale. Either Yale has elected dumbbells to their most prestigious endowed professorships, or even the very best people in the profession—perhaps *especially* the very best people in the profession—are often the subject of competitive, ungenerous, hurtful, and often shrewdly argued criticism. Grant applicants can expect a great deal of the same. Or worse: they may face total indifference to all their hard work.

Though competition can be unpleasant, there are two good things about it. One is that criticism is not always intended to be hurtful, and if you can bring yourself to accept it with good grace, you can use it to improve your work. Take the readers' reports for this book. When I sent a proposal and sample chapter into Yale University Press, one of the outside readers didn't respond at all. Two of the reports, which were clearly written by towering geniuses of impeccable taste and judgment, were very positive. One report expressed completely reasonable doubts and was neutral. And one report was written by a very tiny human being who took out his frustrations over his sorry-ass life by saying mean things about my awesome ideas. Or that's what I thought the first time I read it. At the urging of my brilliant editor, Laura Davulis, I reread the final report and found that it was actually pretty interesting. The reader didn't see things the same way I did, and probably still doesn't. But he or she did have some very useful ideas. I realized it was foolish of me to have been upset and hurt. Based on various criticisms in all the reports, but especially those in the final one, I made substantial changes to the proposal and sample chapter, and the book was accepted for publication. Thanks, reader number four!

Many grant competitions, like the Fulbright-Hays dissertation research grant, let you apply to see readers' reports after the competition is over. You should do so, whether you win or lose. You will learn from them. Even when the criticism is intended to be hurtful, you can still put it to positive use. As in sports, winning the competition is great, but the process of trying to win has collateral benefits, and can make you a better competitor and better person.

The second good thing about harsh competition is that winning in the face of it will be more meaningful, and confer greater joy, than the many

A's you've received in classes throughout your career. When only 10 percent, or 1 percent, of applicants' projects can be funded, there is no possibility for grade inflation. The validation of one's hard work that comes with winning a grant is thus intensely satisfying, offering a shot of confidence that can launch you on new creative odysseys, and a thrill that can energize you for—you guessed it—your next round of grant applications.

Chapter 2

BE AMBITIOUS

When I was in graduate school I had a surreal experience in which every action I took provoked an utterly unexpected reaction from the people I was working with, and all the surprises were pleasant ones. Having followed the controversies around the passage of the North American Free Trade Agreement (NAFTA), I had the idea that international trade was the most important geopolitical issue facing Latin America, and that it would be interesting to get people together to talk about it across disciplinary lines. People in the history and anthropology departments tended to see trade deals like NAFTA as harmful to workers. People in political science and economics tended to see them as largely beneficial. At the time, governments throughout the Americas were considering the extension of NAFTA to the rest of the hemisphere under a proposed "Free Trade Area of the Americas," or FTAA. Wouldn't it be interesting, I thought, to bring together people from different sides of the debate to talk about it? There were faculty members and graduate students across the university who were thinking about these issues. All we would need is a conference room, a video projector, some stale cookies, bad coffee, and paper cups, and we could have ourselves a conference.

I broached the idea with my adviser, Gil Joseph, and he liked it. He suggested I talk with Gustav Ranis, a distinguished economist who was the head of the Yale Center for International and Area Studies. Ranis was skeptical at first, saying it would be boring to have only Yale people involved. I countered that, if a small sum of money could be found, we could bring in one or two people from outside the university. That idea also failed to excite him. He said no one would be interested in a small meeting of the kind I was proposing. Which led me to ask: If small was bad, would big be better? A little surprised, the director answered well, yes, as a matter of fact, it would be. When I said that we would need more money for such an event, the director, after thinking it over, responded that, if I could find someone else to chip in, International and Area Studies would contribute ten thousand dollars. After I picked my jaw up off the floor and put my eyeballs back in, I said I would do my best to find other institutions that could help. I sent proposals to Yale's Center for the Study of Globalization, Political Science Department, Economics Department, History Department, Council for Latin American and Iberian Studies, and several other groups, telling them about the nature of the project and the funding that was on offer. To my astonishment, one by one, each of them said yes. I particularly remember my meeting with Jon Butler, then the chair of the History Department. He held up the two-page proposal I had sent and said, "I see a thousand of these things, but this: I think this is important." With the support of the Center for International and Area Studies, I ended up raising close to forty thousand dollars for the conference. It featured experts and politicians from across the hemisphere and culminated in a dinner speech by Ernesto Zedillo, former president of Mexico.

From this and various similar experiences, I have derived the axiom that ambition can be a powerful tool. People want to be involved in big, important projects, not small, insignificant ones. Funding agencies want to change the world for the better, and those who want their money must show them how the project under consideration will rock the world.

But the implications of the ambition principle for those seeking money for research projects are complicated. It is easy to claim that your project is going to rock the world. It is difficult to persuade skeptical readers that it will indeed do so. This task is made doubly difficult by a countervailing expectation that your project be narrow enough to be completed in a year or less.

How does one put together a proposal that is at once ambitious and narrow? Here is how I begin: if there is a project that I think has potential, I try to describe it to myself, and to friends whose views I respect, in an ordinary conversation. If I can't describe it in a way that makes it interesting to nonspecialists, I know it needs work. For example, I am now working on a project on the conquest of northern Mexico in the late sixteenth century. I tell people this story is interesting for several reasons. It is an amazing tale, based on rich and largely untapped primary sources, that includes both extreme violence and cultural creativity. The war to conquer Mexico's near north had a big, long-term impact on racial identities in New Spain and, later, Mexico. During this war, Europeans and Native peoples fought as allies on a larger scale than ever before. And the conflict resulted in the extermination of many of Mexico's nomadic Indian groups—a genocide that has yet to garner much attention by historians of genocide, race war, and colonial Mexico. My hope, when I describe my work, is to show how a narrowly conceived research project on a seemingly remote subject will have wide-ranging implications for scholars in many fields. So far, this argument has persuaded several grant-making institutions, and I hope it persuades readers when the book is published.

You can try this same approach for testing your research topics. Come up with a description of your project that is straightforward and succinct—perhaps three or four sentences. Tell as many people about it as you can. If one person rolls his eyes and says, "Wow. Who could possibly care?" you should try it on someone else and see if it elicits the same reaction. If several people agree that your project is boring, you should go back to the drawing board. But if other people say, "Wow! That's fascinating! Tell me more!," then that first reaction probably came from someone who is either not very nice, not very smart, or has some sort of axe to grind. Keep on telling people about your project, and try to refine and polish your short, paragraph-length version for maximum impact.

To take one memorable example of a narrow project revealing itself to be ambitious, consider the case of Rowan Steineker, a doctoral student in history at the University of Oklahoma. In my grant-writing workshop for graduate students, Steinecker talked about a project she was working on dealing with the life of a white schoolteacher in an indigenous community in Missouri. At first, the project sounded too narrow in scope to me, and thus difficult to fund. It seemed too easy to say, "Who cares?" But in dialogue with the group, Steineker made it clear that the story of this schoolteacher had deep implications for the way we understand native peoples and their interactions with state-sponsored education programs, most of which were explicitly geared for the eradication of native cultures. During this time, Indian boarding schools were weapons of mass cultural destruction. By offering a fine-brush portrait of this teacher's life and her interactions with the native community she lived in, Steineker showed that both the cultural agenda of educators and the political intelligence of native peoples were vastly more flexible than most readers would expect, demonstrating that the state and native peoples could adapt to one another creatively. Steineker's project revealed a bright, hopeful thread running through the grim tapestry of government malevolence and native suffering that is American Indian history. So promising was this project that its author recently earned a dissertation completion grant from the National Academy of Education worth $27,500.

To take another example of a project that combines narrow focus with broad ambition, consider Ramie Targoff's brilliant *Posthumous Love: Eros and the Afterlife in Renaissance England.* This study of Renaissance English love poetry turns on a fascinating observation: Italian poets of the Renaissance followed the ancient Romans in imagining that the love of husbands and wives continued into the afterlife. English Renaissance poets insisted that the opposite was the case. They assumed that love between mortals was itself mortal and would not carry on in heaven—or hell, as it does for the star-crossed lovers Paolo and Francesca in Dante's *Inferno.* So, the subject matter—Renaissance love poetry concerned with life, mortality, and afterlife—is carefully limited. Yet the questions Targoff addresses are of wide-ranging interest to students of literature, history, and religion. Did the difference between Italy and England stem from the fact that one was mostly Catholic and the other mostly Protestant? Or were differing ideas about love and the afterlife poetic, aesthetic, or philosophical? These are profound questions about deep feelings and intense religious politics. Beyond that, the subject is interesting not only to scholars, but to us all. Anyone who has seen the Etruscan matrimonial sarcophagi that Targoff describes, with their gorgeous marble sculptures of married couples enjoying paradise together in the afterlife, has been struck by their deeply foreign, yet moving, vision of married love. By drawing our attention to the world's most brilliant writing on the world's most poignant subject matter, the book illuminates in new ways the preoccupations of scholars and nonscholars alike. The project is narrow in scope but broad in ambition. The book's acknowledgments reveal that Targoff spent two years on leave in Italy working on it, courtesy of the ACLS, the John Simon Guggenheim Foundation, and the American Academy in Rome. It is exactly the kind of focused but implication-rich project that funding agencies love.[1]

A great way to measure the viability of any grant proposal is to gauge how effectively it dramatizes the importance of a narrowly defined topic. Research grants are for projects that are big and ambitious, yet well-defined. These projects must have the potential to change people's minds about issues that are important beyond the immediate scope of the applicant's research. If you are not ambitious, you exclude yourself from the competition before you've entered it. This is another instance in which the process of applying for grants forces you to work harder, dream bigger, think more deeply, and, in general, become a better intellectual than you were before. That's reason enough to apply.

Chapter 3

ASSEMBLE A TEAM

When I read a scholarly book for the first time, I always start by looking at the cover, the illustrations, the footnotes, and the acknowledgments. The acknowledgments are usually the most interesting. They tell you where the author comes from, who has trained him, what grants he's gotten, which archives he's gone to, and hints about his love life. Acknowledgments are, I'm sorry to say, often more interesting than the rest of the book. They also implicitly make an important point: all scholarship is done by a team. Even when a book or article lists a single author, there is always a vast network of institutions, publishers, editors, teachers, family members, and friends who have assisted in the creation of the work you hold in your hands. Walt Whitman said of *Leaves of Grass*, "Who touches this book touches a man." We might say, "Who touches this book (or dissertation or article) touches a scholarly community."[1]

For those who want to produce scholarship, the upshot is that you need to assemble a team of people to support you. You will need both teachers or mentors who will write recommendations for you, and peers whom you can consult, offer help to, and get help from. But how can you recruit and motivate such a support team?

PART 1: RECOMMENDERS

Some years ago, a sociologist named Annette Lareau published a book called *Unequal Childhoods: Class, Race, and Family Life*. It is an account of the cultures of child-rearing among working-class and affluent families. The thesis was that working-class people bring up their children in ways that make it difficult for them to succeed in education, the job market, and life in general. Whereas affluent people are constantly taking their children to band practice and soccer practice and to acting school and actual school, working-class people tend (according to this study) to say simply, "go outside and play." The author enumerated a set of skills and practices that high-end parenting imparts to children that help them advance in life. Key to this skillset is the ability to work with institutions. While working-class parents tend to let their children believe that institutions are looming enemies to be treated with suspicion and fear, affluent parents tell their kids that institutions are complicated but necessary features of everyday life. The study says rich parents make their kids understand that, by being friendly and assertive and politic, they can get from institutions what they need, and can advance within them. These skills are indispensable later on. When the children of wealthy parents want to dispute a low grade, extract a driver's license from the DMV, get a mortgage, obtain a recommendation from a busy teacher, get into college, or rise in the ranks of management, their upbringing gives them a competitive edge.[2]

The reason I don't find this study entirely persuasive is that it pays little attention to all the other conditions that hold poor kids back: the lack of money being the most salient. It's for that reason that, whenever I begin reading a book or article on "the culture of poverty," I think some combination of, "oh no, no not again"; "this had better be good"; and "I'll be very surprised if this isn't an extended exercise in victim-blaming." Time and again conservative social scientists come up with creative reasons to believe that inequality doesn't matter, and that the downtrodden are to blame for their own downtroddenness.

But there is a kernel of truth in the notion that people should learn, preferably at an early age, that institutions can be both implacable enemies and complicated but useful friends. A special combination of patience, persistence, friendliness, organization, and self-control is indispensable to succeeding within them. This is especially true when it comes to getting the letters of recommendation you need in order to obtain research funding.

After too many years of education, it is only now that I've been able to articulate the following law of working within institutions: in your relations with your recommenders, you are mostly their servant, but you are also partly their manager. You are their servant in the sense that you want to do everything you can to do a good job and impress them. You are their servant also in the sense that you must do the legwork necessary to make recommending you easy. Yet at the same time, in subtle ways, you are their manager. Like a manager, you need to state clearly, and well ahead of time, what it is you want your recommenders to do for you. You must give them (discreet, friendly) reminders of what is due on what date. You must politely check their progress and make sure that their work is completed in a timely fashion. And in the end, like a good boss, you must thank them for their work, share credit for your accomplishments, and accept 100 percent of the blame for your failures.

This is a difficult balancing act to perform. The more students I recommend, the more impressed I've become with the sheer variety of ways in which they fail to perform it. I shudder to think about the number of ways I've failed to perform it in my own career. For the most part, people fail to do the right things in their relations with recommenders simply because nobody has told them clearly what to do. So, allow me to do just that. How does one become the best possible servant/manager of your recommenders? Let's start with what not to do. Here is a list of ways to utterly blow it:

- **Start late.** Nobody wants to get this email: "So sorry, professor, but could you send a recommendation letter to this person by noon today?" I've sent that email myself, and I feel gross just thinking about it.
- **Forget that you are the recommender's servant.** Given the exorbitant price of education these days, some students have gotten it into their heads that professors are their underlings. But if you want a good recommendation, treating your professor with contempt will be counterproductive.
- **Forget that you are the recommender's manager.** You, not your recommender, are responsible for making sure the letter arrives at its destination on time. Delegating the task to your recommender and then forgetting about it presumes too much. Your recommenders need your attention, help, and encouragement.

- **Do weak, mailed-in work.** Do not underperform in the classes you take and assignments you submit to the professor/recommender. Not much explanation needed here.

Defining how not to do it makes it all the easier to define how to do it well:

- **Start early.** If you've taken a class with Professor X, participated in a seminar when she was present, or written a book or article on which she has commented favorably, write her an email that goes something like this:

Dear [professor's name],

It was such a pleasure to work with you in [context]. I would be so honored if you could write a letter of recommendation for me. If you can't, I completely understand. I realize you have many people asking you for letters, and much else on your agenda.

But if you are willing and able, the letter needs to be sent to [location] by [date about three months from now]. The fellowship I am applying for is for [name and purpose of fellowship]. I'll send you my résumé, project description, and samples of my work if you would like to see them.

Thanks so much for your time. Whatever happens, I look forward to talking again about [enumerate shared interests].

Best wishes,

[your name]

You're obviously going to want to use your own words, but you should similarly try to be friendly, conversational, and respectful of the professor while projecting a sense of self-respect. Emphasize the interests you share with the potential letter writer, and place your request in the context of an ongoing intellectual exchange. I once asked for a letter from a professor I greatly admired, whose works I had read, but with whom I had never taken any classes. He said no. He had too many students of his own competing for the same funds. I nevertheless continued to correspond with him about our shared interests. He has never written a letter for me, but he has become one of my most valued and trusted advisers, and we correspond and share work to this day. When, by contrast, students show up only when they need something and disappear thereafter, it is always a little depressing to letter writers. The key is to plan far in advance and do everything you can to make recommending you easy.

- **Remember you are the recommender's servant.** Be prompt, efficient, friendly, and respectful; work hard; and be willing to disappear the moment you get the sense the recommender has other things to attend to. The recommender will probably be happy to know you admire her work and ideas, and that you really enjoy working on related topics. She probably will not be interested in gifts or fulsome flattery, so avoid at all costs naming her queen of her scholarly universe, or the sexiest creature you've likely ever laid eyes on (a whole other set of issues there).

  You want the recommender to be able to say of you what biologist E. O. Wilson writes of his student Corrie Saux Moreau in *Letters to a Young Scientist*: "There was no bravado in Corrie, no trace of overweening pride, no pretension. She was a quiet, serene enthusiast. As it turned out, she was also an open, helpful friend to fellow students and others around her. . . . I wanted her to succeed, and while I did not join her as a collaborator, I found the funds to set up her laboratory." Young Moreau had clearly hit the sweet spot of hard work, enthusiasm, self-control, and respectfulness of the mentor's work. You should try to do the same.[3]

- **Remember you are the recommender's manager.** Once the recommender says yes, provide her with everything she'll need to recommend you: your résumé, project description, a sample of your work, and a list of the places the letter needs to be sent with brief descriptions of the nature of the fellowships you are applying for. If the letter needs to be sent by snail mail, provide stamped, addressed envelopes. Ask if there is anything else you can provide. About a week ahead of the due date, let the recommender know that the deadline is approaching. Once you've sent all your materials in, contact the foundation or other grant-offering organization to ask if all your letters have been received. If they have not, gently contact your recommender to let her know her letter is missing. You might write something like this:

Dear Professor X,

I've just finished sending all my materials to the Y Foundation, and I understand that for some reason, probably technical, they have yet to receive your letter. In case you need it, here is the address the letter should be sent to, and the date by which it should arrive: [insert here the mailing address or URL, as well as the due date]. So sorry for the bother, and MANY thanks once again for supporting me. I know you receive many requests like mine, and I'm very grateful for the help.

Cordial regards,

[your name]

Here once again, you want to make yourself easy to recommend. This means providing all the materials and information the recommender needs. It also means behaving in such a way that the recommender has positive associations with the idea of recommending you. I once had a graduate student drive up behind me while I was riding my bike and honk his horn, thus scaring me out of my wits. Once he had pulled over and gotten out of the car, he walked up, asked me for a recommendation, and went on to inform me that he hadn't read a single one of the books that I had suggested months earlier he read for his work. In other words, he both nearly caused my death, and did not accept the help on his work that I had offered and that he badly needed. When I wrote the letter, I did my best to suppress my mixed feelings: the letter I wrote was strongly positive and focused on the student's many virtues. Nevertheless, you should not try to make it an unpleasant chore for your recommenders to write for you.

- Do strong, timely, innovative work. The case of Corrie Saux Moreau, mentioned earlier, is instructive. She came to E. O. Wilson late in his teaching career and displayed tremendous enthusiasm for the study of ants, for which Wilson is famous. (She did so not only by being passionately committed to the pursuit of myrmecological knowledge, but also by tattooing large images of ants on her person.) Moreau performed brilliantly in her courses, took setbacks in stride, laid out ambitious plans, consulted Wilson from time to time, and accomplished an enormous amount on her own. For all these reasons she was easy to recommend. She now holds dual positions at the

University of Chicago and the Field Museum of Natural History. Even without the body art, hers is a good model to follow.

Whom should you ask? There are generally two qualities that you want your recommenders to have: they should be respected in their field, and they should know and support your work. Unfortunately, those two qualities are often mutually repelling. Many famous geniuses will think, or know, nothing of your work. And many of those who support you may fall into the category of those indispensable people who are wonderful teachers and totally unknown in their fields. So how do we square the circle? Here is how I think about it: plot your possible recommenders on the graph below.

		1	2	3	4	5	6	7	8	9	10
Revered in	10										X
her field	9						X	X			
	8								X		
	7										
	6		X					X			
	5										
	4		X								X
	3										
Totally	2						X	X			
Unknown	1	2	3	4	5	6	7	8	9	10

Doesn't know you from Adam	**Loves your work**

If the X axis represents support for your work and the Y axis represents fame, you generally want your recommenders to fall as close to the upper right corner of the graph as possible. Letters from a famous person who doesn't know you from Adam (or Eve) are unhelpful. So are those from nobodies who worship the ground you walk on. If, unbeknownst to you, the famous person does have an opinion about you, and it is negative, her letter can be even more damaging to your case than a semiliterate encomium from the yoga instructor with whom you are having an affair. I've seen both kinds of letter. A thorough, detailed, forcefully written recommendation from a little-known younger professor, however, can be very persuasive. I've written such a letter for an undergraduate, and I like to think it had some role in her admission to graduate school at Yale. She was an amazing powerhouse, but the admissions committee may not have recognized that in the absence of my letter. In addition, a cursory but positive letter from the pope of your field can also carry much weight. The pope's name, the fact that he took the time to write the recommendation, the very letterhead he uses, can all cast a powerful spell.

It is not that there is no right or wrong way to select your recommenders. It's more that there are many varieties of both right and wrong. Use your wit. Have conversations with the people you would like to recommend you. Pay close attention to what they say about your work. Zealously follow their advice and let your work show that they have influenced you.

PART 2: PEERS

Be a giver. For all those who want to succeed in academia, business, and life, that is the advice of young Wharton School dynamo Adam Grant, whose rocketlike success is as powerful a piece of evidence for his thesis as are the reams of data he provides to support it. Grant argues that in most institutions, there are three kinds of people: givers, matchers, and takers. Matchers are the largest group. They do unto others as others do unto them: "You help me, I help you." A simple and time-tested strategy if ever there was one. There is exactly nothing wrong with it. Takers are a smaller group. Their philosophy is: "You help me, I screw you." We've all met them. They're out there. Their rise, when it occurs, is always watched with hatred and envy by all the people they've trampled on. Recipients of their trampling sometimes think that all successful people are takers. But this blinds them to the existence of the third group, which is also small: givers. Their modus operandi is: "I help you, and you do as you please. If you help me, great! If you don't, no problem! But the fact is, I just like helping people, and oddly enough, doing so has somehow eventuated in my becoming very successful indeed. The irony!"[4]

Grant's argument is that the rise of the givers is not a bit ironic, and that everyone can do well by doing good. The premise of Grant's claim is that the economy has changed in deep ways. People used to have long, stable careers in large, hierarchical organizations. Today, people's jobs are in a continual state of flux. Organizations are flat, collaboration is ubiquitous, and interdependence is the rule. In jobs where one is frequently working as part of a team, people who are generous to others stand out. Their behavior redounds to the benefit of their coworkers. The more people a giver has helped, the better his reputation gets. More and more people are willing to respect, support, and promote him. Grant uses a wonderful neologism to describe the state that givers live in: pronoia. Paranoid people are constantly afraid that the world is conspiring against them. Givers, who have an ever-increasing cohort of peers they've helped, enjoy pronoia. Pronoia is a state in which one suspects, with reason, that the world is conspiring to help and support one. Givers are pronoid.

There are two common objections raised by Grant's critics. One is that givers spend so much time helping others that they don't have time to help themselves, and for this reason they tend to fall behind. Grant counters with data from numerous studies indicating that the best performers in some of the world's most successful organizations are givers. They frequently use their power to help others, so people are more than willing to help and promote them. The second objection people raise is that takers are often successful. Grant acknowledges that possibility. But he shows many instances in which being a taker leads to short-term prosperity and long-term suffering. The success of takers is fragile because so many people are gunning for them. The success of givers is robust because so many people want them to prosper.

When applying for grants, the advantages of being a giver and disadvantages of being a taker are stark. Say, for instance, you find out about a grant for which you and several of your peers are eligible. If you fail to tell your peers about it, the likelihood that you will get the grant may rise infinitesimally, since fewer applicants means a greater probability of success. To translate a Mexican proverb, the fewer donkeys there are, the more corn cobs each one gets ("Entre menos burros, más olotes"). But by keeping this grant secret, the likelihood that you will alienate your peers increases dramatically. They'll probably find out about the grant anyway, and they may well discover that you knew about it, especially if you do end up getting it—and will not be inclined to help you in the future. By contrast, if you do tell your peers about the grant, the chance that you will get it will decrease by a tiny amount, while the chances that your peers will be inclined to help you will go up by a lot. The mix of costs and benefits associated with being a giver is clearly more attractive than those of being a taker. Over time, having a group of peers you trust, whom you have helped, and who want to help you is enormously valuable as you all work to apply for grants. In particular, you can form a grant-writing group that will offer opportunities to help and be helped by your peers, through sharing information, offering constructive criticism, and encouragement when times are tough and grants fall through.

Whatever success I've enjoyed in life has come about in large part because I've been taught by generous givers with enormously extensive accomplishments. To a person, these mentors are serial givers of the first order, and they have all risen to the pinnacles of their professions. Follow their example. Play the long game. As an anthropologist once told me, initiate long cycles of reciprocity. Be a giver. You won't regret it.

A warning and an observation about building your team: academia is competitive, and with competition come stress and insecurity. Different people handle stress and insecurity in different ways. When you add immaturity to the mix, the brew can become toxic. I've known deeply immature people who are well into their fifties and are very successful. What I mean by immature is that they are smugly focused on themselves, judge others harshly but themselves leniently, are pathetically dependent on praise, and are deeply pained by other people's success. Whether you call it immaturity, being a taker, or just being a garden-variety jerk, this condition, like undiagnosed Asperger syndrome, is endemic to the academic trade.

Destructively immature people are to be avoided when you are assembling your team of peers. But how do you identify them? There are two quotations I've found useful in answering this question. One I discovered in college and it has never led me wrong. The novelist William S. Burroughs once said, "If, after spending time with a person, you feel as though you've lost a quart of plasma, avoid that person in the future." It's funny because it's true. Very often, when people are being awful, they try to hide it. You sense their awfulness emotionally long before you understand it mentally. So trust your gut feeling. If someone is bringing you down, they are probably doing it on purpose. If not, they are doing it because that is the only way they know how to interact with others. The good news is, there's no need to figure out what is going on in your case. Just follow Saint Bill's advice and avoid that person in the future.[5]

The other quotation says more or less the same thing, but in a different way. It comes from a remarkable book that must have been a publisher's dream come true when the manuscript came in over the transom. It's called *The Gift of Fear*, by Gavin de Becker. It is in essence a self-help book, but it reads like a true-crime thriller to rival Truman Capote's *In Cold Blood*. De Becker is a personal security expert with broad experience defending prominent people, including Hollywood movie stars and several justices of the U.S. Supreme Court. De Becker's trade is figuring out which threats of violence are serious and which are not. Crazy people often send letters to people like Ruth Bader Ginsburg threatening them with death, dismemberment, and worse. Of these threats, 99 percent are not serious. The trick is identifying the 1 percent that are.[6]

De Becker argues that there are certain warning signals that seriously violent people unconsciously emit and that can be detected by the well-trained observer. These signals include refusing to take no for an answer, offering unsolicited help, and what de Becker calls "Forced Teaming"—for example, "Hey, we're both stuck in the middle of nowhere in the rain, let's team up and figure it out. Just get into the back of my van and we can talk about it." De Becker also offers the observation that everyone he's ever met who has been assaulted says afterward, "I had a bad feeling about that situation." He goes on to write, "Since there are almost always warning signs of violence, most people can later recount what they missed." Some may dismiss de Becker's thesis as victim-blaming. But I don't. The attacker still bears all the blame. Moreover, de Becker's thesis has an upside, and the critics' position has a downside, that we should pay attention to: if people are intuitively sensitive to threats, then it is possible to train yourself to respect your own intuitions and so avoid potentially violent situations. Dismissing de Becker as a victim-blamer leads to the fatalistic conclusion that there is nothing you can do to protect yourself; you might as well just let yourself be victimized.

Physical violence among academics does sometimes happen, but that's not what I'm writing about. I'm referring to *professional* violence: when someone dismisses, pooh-poohs, undermines, frustrates, or steals others' work. Odd combinations of these behaviors can occur as well: for example, "Your work is so bad that I'm going to steal it and pass it off as my own." Such professional aggression is distressingly common. But like physical violence, there are almost always warning signs that precede professional violence. In fact, many perpetrators announce to the world, over and over again, that they are about to commit some form of unpleasantness. For instance, if you have a colleague who habitually implies that all those who disagree with him are either stupid or insane, that's a pretty good indicator that you don't want him in your writing group. If someone always seems to be saying that all scholarship sucks and nothing is good, you know what to do. If someone you are having a conversation with expresses contempt for things that you say you find exciting, compelling, or novel, steer clear.

I once made an attempt at small talk with one such person when I crossed paths with him in a coffee shop. I said, "Guess what: I just learned that blond roast actually has *more* caffeine than dark roast. I thought it was the other way around!" He scoffed and said, "Pfft! I've known that for twenty years." You can imagine what he'd say about my latest book idea. I'm reminded of a similar exchange when, during a conversation with a prominent expert on Buddhism, of all things, I praised a frittata I had recently ordered at a restaurant. "What?" he angrily replied, "A *frittata!* How could that possibly be so great? All you have to do is take leftovers and sauté them with eggs!" Ooo-kaayy, I thought. Just trying to make conversation here. Like venomous puffer fish, inflating themselves and displaying their spikes, such people are warning you to swim in the other direction. You can usually tell intuitively those whom you should avoid working with. Trust your instincts.

Positive intuition is equally important. Gilbert Joseph of Yale, Tom Conley of Harvard, Jorge Cañizares-Esguerra of University of Texas at Austin, and several other people I know have a magical power I wish I had. Whenever I have a conversation with them, I come away more excited about my own work, about their work, and about life in general. Such people are rare birds indeed. Their generosity and enthusiasm are a powerful source of intellectual energy for everyone they work with. If a friend or peer has a talent for perceptive listening and an infectious enthusiasm for new ideas, by all means, include her in your writing group and hope she says yes. Such people are often in heavy demand. Here once again, it may be possible to attract such people into your intellectual orbit. But it's more important to strive to be such a person. This is yet another way grant writing can be good for the soul. Give freely and you shall receive.

Part II

INGREDIENTS

Chapter 4

CRAFT A COMPELLING QUESTION

All grant makers have the same goal: a finished product about which they can proudly say, "Our money helped produced this." They also want to know how you'll prove whether the project is a success. One very effective way of answering these questions is to produce a question of your own—a special kind of question. The historian Margaret Chowning describes it as a simple question with a complicated answer. In a seminar I took with John Mack Faragher, he memorably described the research question as a "can opener" with which you take the lid off your sources.[1]

How do you produce this kind of question? Oops: I've just done it without realizing it. The question of where good research questions come from is itself just the kind of question you need. It can be stated simply, yet it leads to fascinating places. I produced it by thinking out loud about something that puzzles and interests me. That is one place to start looking for a viable research question: think out loud about something you don't quite understand and want to know more about.

Here is another approach: consider the best research in your field, the books and articles that have won awards and influenced people. In my fields, Latin American, Native American, and borderlands history, here are some such works:

Charles Gibson, *The Aztecs under Spanish Rule: A History of the Indians of the Valley of Mexico, 1519–1810* (Stanford, CA: Stanford University Press, 1964).

Stuart Schwartz, *All Can Be Saved: Religious Tolerance and Salvation in the Iberian Atlantic World* (New Haven: Yale University Press, 2009).

William Taylor, *Magistrates of the Sacred: Parish Priests and Indian Parishioners in Eighteenth Century Mexico* (Stanford, CA: Stanford University Press, 1999).

John Tutino, *Making a New World: Founding Capitalism in the Bajío and Spanish North America* (Durham, NC: Duke University Press, 2011).

Richard White, *The Middle Ground: Indians, Empires, and Republics in the Great Lakes region, 1650–1815* (Cambridge, UK: Cambridge University Press, 1991).

You can undoubtedly think of many for your field. Now, for each of these books and articles, try to state as simply as possible the question that each of them answers. Here is my attempt.

Gibson, *Aztecs*. How did the Aztecs adapt to life in the Spanish empire?

Schwartz, *All*. Were ordinary people in the Iberian empires tolerant of other religious groups, and if so, when, how, and why?

Taylor, *Magistrates*. What can the identities, careers, ideas, and acts of Mexico's parish priests tell us about the political change in eighteenth-century Mexico?

Tutino, *Making*. What was the nature of New Spain's economy, and how did it influence other economies of the Atlantic World?

White, *Middle*. How did peoples of disparate ethnicities, languages, and cultures coexist in the Great Lakes region, where the state and rule of law were all but absent?

Each of these books can be thought of as answering a simple question in complex ways. Thinking about both the question and the answers together allows us to see the topic "synoptically," to use one of Taylor's favorite terms. That is, we can see both the big picture and detail, the forest and the trees, the map and the territory. Your proposal should provide the reader with this kind of synoptic vision. One of the most powerful ways of doing that is to formulate a short and powerful research question, then offer a sampling of your answers to it.

Before we move on from the questions posed by my list of authors, there is more that we can do with them. As you try to think up your own research questions, you can simply transport the questions other scholars have asked to a different place, time, and context and see what you come up with. You can put a different twist on the questions. You can argue that each of them is a good question but is answered incorrectly by the authority who first posed it. You can argue that, as the French say, the question is *mal posée*, and that we should approach the same topic from a different angle. These are very basic mental exercises, but they lead us into fascinating and unexpected territory. They also allow us to frame problems in useful ways. Framing is indispensable for the creation of a good research project. By defining exactly what lies within the scope of your project and what lies outside of it, you let the grant proposal evaluator know what you are going to do with the foundation's money.

So let's play with the research questions posed by the brilliant authors in the books I've listed.

- Gibson, *Aztecs*. How did the Aztecs adapt to life in the Spanish empire?
  - How did the Mayas adapt to life in the Spanish empire?
  - Did nonsedentary peoples fare better or worse than the sedentary Aztecs under Spanish rule?
  - Did the Spanish really "rule" their empire?
- Schwartz, *All*. Were ordinary people in the Iberian empires tolerant of other religious groups, and if so, why and how?
  - Do the Inquisitorial Archives of France and its colonies reveal similar patterns of vernacular religious tolerance?
  - Was the Chinese empire more or less religiously tolerant than the Spanish and Portuguese empires were?
  - When and where were people most intolerant in the Iberian imperial worlds?
- Taylor, *Magistrates*. What can the identities, careers, ideas, and actions of Mexico's parish priests tell us about the political change in eighteenth-century Mexico?
  - Can Taylor's method be applied to other social groups, such as Inquisition judges, bishops, or native town councilmen?
  - Were parish priests as critical a social group in Brazil as in New Spain?

- ○ How did Jesuits differ from secular priests in their attitudes and role in eighteenth-century New Spain?
- Tutino, *Making*. What was the nature of colonial Mexico's economy, and how did it influence other economies of the Atlantic World?
  - ○ Does economics offer the most powerful tools to examine Mexican society in the colonial period, or might anthropology get us further?
  - ○ Does Tutino define capitalism adequately, or might a better definition reveal a different picture of Mexican economic development?
  - ○ Was Mexican economic thought as influential abroad as Tutino claims?
- White, *Middle*. How did peoples of disparate ethnicity, language, and culture coexist in the Great Lakes Region, where the state and rule of law were all but absent?
  - ○ Was there a "middle ground" in Roman North Africa?
  - ○ Was there a "middle ground" in colonial Pennsylvania?
  - ○ Was the Great Lakes region as "middle" a "ground" as White thinks?

Each of these outstanding works provides examples and ideas that enable research elsewhere. Indeed, many of the questions I've derived from them have been asked, and brilliantly answered. James Merrell's *Into the American Woods* asks whether colonial Pennsylvania hosted a middle ground, and answers, in coruscating detail, "not really." Nancy Farriss's *Maya Society under Colonial Rule* adapts Gibson's questions to the native peoples of Chiapas, Yucatán, and Guatemala.[2]

If you are struggling to articulate your own research question, select the five works of scholarship you find most inspiring. Think about each for a moment, and then try and state the question that book or article is trying to answer. State it as simply as possible. Brainstorm on it. Produce five alternative questions by slightly altering the question you began with. Think about where else the books' questions might work. Think about how they might yield more interesting answers. Pretty soon you will have a list of twenty-five questions you can select among for your proposal.

Let's look at some influential books of recent years in anthropology and political science, the questions they seek to answer, and some ways that researchers could adapt those questions to their own curiosities.

- Robert A. Dahl, *How Democratic Is the American Constitution?* (New Haven: Yale University Press, 2003). Um . . . what he said.

- How democratic is the constitution of France?
- How often do the most democratic constitutions lead to the most democratic societies?
- Under what conditions do countries adopt anti-democratic constitutions?

- Matthew C. Gutmann, *The Meanings of Macho: Being a Man in Mexico* (Berkeley: University of California Press, 1996). How do Mexican men see themselves, behave as fathers, treat women, and talk about sex?
  - Are there many kinds of macho, some praiseworthy and others not?
  - Are Japanese men macho?
  - Are Mexican women ever praised as *machas?* Under what circumstances and why?

- James C. Scott, *The Art of Not Being Governed: An Anarchist History of Highland Southeast Asia* (New Haven: Yale University Press, 2010). Why would people deliberately strive to remain beyond the reach of state power?
  - Are the same patterns of flight from the state seen in the mountains of Central Europe as in the highlands of Southeast Asia?
  - Are the reasons people seek to escape state control in the jungles of Bolivia different from the catalysts for flight in Southeast Asia?
  - What motivates the people who do not flee, but rather seek protection from the state in Southeast Asia?
  - Do states in Southeast Asia use only coercion to keep people under control? Or do they also seduce them into sacrificing their freedom with incentives?

- Theda Skocpol and Vanessa Williamson, *The Tea Party and the Making of Republican Conservatism* (New York: Oxford University Press, 2013). Who are the members of the Republican Tea Party Movement, and what do they want?
  - Is there an equivalent movement on the left wing of American politics? Why? Why not?
  - Are generational differences as important to this movement as the authors believe?
  - Is the Tea Party new, or just the latest iteration of an old pattern in American politics?
  - How do right-wing populist movements in Europe differ from the Tea Party Movement?

No matter what field you work in, the exercise of defining the research questions of the best work you know can get you started on an interesting new path.

Another important thing to think about are so-called bad research questions. These generally are bad not because they are not interesting, but because no amount of research can answer them. What is the nature of human intention? What would Plato have made of the iPhone? How were homosexuals treated among preliterate Basques five thousand years ago? All of these questions are fascinating to consider. But either because there is no extant evidence that can answer them, or because the problem is so profound that no number of lifetimes would suffice to answer them, they are what I would consider bad research questions.

Bad research questions are not without their uses, however. If they can be narrowed or reframed, they can often be swiftly transformed from bad research questions into very good ones indeed. What are the weaknesses in W. V. O. Quine's ideas about the nature of human intention? How are gays treated among the Basques today? Are there significant parallels between the cognitive techniques of Socratic reasoning and those of computer programming? These are questions that, by virtue of being narrow, are sharp, and so have the power to penetrate to the heart of things.

Chapter 5

BRAINSTORM WITHIN YOUR SUBJECT

Here's an unpleasant fact about research grants: you have to do a good deal of research before anyone gives you money to do research. Not fair. This is a big part of why people who get one grant tend to get more: they've already had time to find potential sources of funding and ponder projects they can base on those grant makers' criteria. They also may have had time to publish research that proves they are able to put grants to good use. But here's the thing: foundations are giving out money. They have to make the work of selection easier in any way they can, in order to avoid being overwhelmed by applications. Beyond that, selecting projects that are in large part already done both insures that their money will be well spent, and forms a barrier to entry to the competition. The decisions they make are very difficult. There are far more worthy projects out there than they can fund. They welcome anything that makes it easier to separate the wheat from the chaff.

For you, the upshot is clear: do everything you can to make yourself difficult to eliminate. We'll be discussing various ways to avoid mistakes that can make you easy to eliminate. But for the moment, let's focus on the question of subject matter. You have to have identified the subjects of your research long before you ask for money to examine them. Very generally:

- Historians will focus on printed and manuscript documents.
- Literary scholars will identify some writer, text, or group of texts.
- Art historians will zero in on one or more artists or works of art.
- Philosophers will look at a conceptual problem or group of texts that address it.
- Political scientists will seek out a puzzle in government or policy.
- Anthropologists will consider a culture or set of cultural practices.
- Economists will go after a problem in finance, policy, or economic behavior.

These are gross oversimplifications. But in all these disciplines, there is a researcher and an object of research. The grant writer must identify the object of research very specifically, precisely defining its characteristics and limitations. And in order to do that, he or she has to do a significant amount of preliminary research and reading.

This requirement represents both an obstacle and an opportunity. Many people will not have the time, drive, funding, or wit to do this preliminary work. Doing it will be one way to distinguish yourself from the field of applicants. But how? If you are an undergraduate, graduate student, or recently minted Ph.D., the best place to start is your coursework. The research papers you've written are a gold mine. Comb through them for ideas that you want to explore further. See if there are unfinished analyses, or ideas that can be pushed further, in old papers you've written. Comb through the notes you've taken. If you've been out of graduate school for a number of years, rethink the conference presentations you've given, lectures you've written, lesson plans you've laid out, and assignments you've given your students. There is always material there that needs further exploration. Because you've already thought about these topics, you've already begun your journey.

For instance, in my field, colonial Latin American history, a book that professors are continually raiding for information for their survey lectures is *The First America: The Spanish Monarchy, Creole Patriots, and the Liberal State, 1492–1866*, by D. A. Brading. The book is nominally about how Spanish Americans born in the New World established a sense of their own social identity. Brading's methods are not complicated, but his results are impressive. He selected several hundred of the historical, political, and scientific works published in, or on, Spanish America between 1492 and 1866, put them in chronological order, and perused them all. He then wrote a 750-page narrative analysis of them, focusing on certain important themes, but following his ideas wherever they took him, and writing it all up in sparkling prose. I've now read it cover to cover twice. It is wonderful.[1]

One can spin an infinite number of research projects out of this extraordinary tome. For instance, there are many thinkers whom Brading was not able to look at in depth, whose works he may have understood imperfectly, and about whom there is a great deal more to write. One could read more deeply in the writings of any of these thinkers than Brading did, think about how that reading differs from Brading's, and make that the core of a research project. One could simply redo all of Brading's research and focus on themes different from those he selected: instead of creole patriotism, you could focus on social class, or family, changing notions of the nature of the afterlife. One could design a similar research project for writers based in the French empire rather than the Spanish one. One could extend the project from 1866 to 1966. The possibilities are limitless. It would be easy to find similar books in other fields—big, authoritative studies that are useful for lecture-writing and leave the reader both stimulated and hungry for more.

Far more difficult than finding some interesting topic to write about is the task of limiting and framing it. The biologist E. O. Wilson has a beautiful description of the way scientists frame their experiments that is useful here. Scientists, he says, are interested in complexity, so they try "to find points of entry into otherwise impenetrably complex systems." The better to do so, Wilson instructs his readers to

> Let your mind travel around the system. Pose an interesting question about it. Break the question down and visualize the elements and questions it implies. Think out alternative conceivable answers. Phrase them so that a reasonable amount of evidence makes a clear-cut choice possible. If too many conceptual difficulties are encountered, back off. Search for another question. When you finally hit a soft spot, search for the model system—say a controlled emission in particle physics or a fast-breeding organism in genetics—on which decisive experiments can be most easily conducted. Become thoroughly familiar—no, better, become obsessed—with the system. Love the details, the feel of all of them, for their own

sake. Design the experiment so that no matter what the result, the answer to the question will be convincing. Use the result to press on to new questions, new systems. Depending on how far others have already gone in this sequence (and always keep in mind, you must give them complete credit), you may enter it at any point along the way.[2]

There are bound to be differences between Wilson's methods and yours. But the similarities are more salient. If you substitute your subject matter for Wilson's "systems," these similarities become clearer. Whether your work focuses on a body of archival documents, a group of literary or philosophical texts, a small community or group of communities, or an institution of government, you should follow Wilson's advice: "let your mind travel around" it, "pose an interesting question about it," "become obsessed" with it, and "love the details, the feel of them, for their own sake." Especially valuable is his advice to "back off" when you run into difficulties, and to pose your question in such a way that a "reasonable amount of evidence makes a clear-cut choice possible." Generally speaking, scholars in the humanities and social sciences don't conduct experiments. But they do conduct research, and they do need to ask interesting questions that can be answered by a reasonable amount of evidence.

A reasonable amount of evidence is an amount you can envision collecting in the period of the grant. You should be as specific as possible in describing it. Here's one way to ensure that no one will give you a dime: write "I plan to go to France and go to as many archives as possible and collect documents on the French Revolution." This is vague, sweeping, and unfocused. Here's another way that will give you a far better shot at grant money: "For my study of policing in revolutionary France, I plan to go to the Archives de la Préfecture de Police (in Le Pré-Saint-Gervais) and the Archives municipales de Dieppe, both of which have a remarkably continuous record of police activity from 1789 to 1820. Particularly rich are the Dieppe files in section D I 6, (municipalité, séances de 28 germinal, 4 et 23 floréal et 19 messidor an III), and the prefecture files A.P.P. A/A 98 to 197. A two-month stay in each location will suffice to make a thorough study of the relevant documents." This research plan is ambitious but focused, and lets the reader know exactly what you plan to do with the grant money. Scholars in all fields of the social sciences and humanities have ways of identifying their source material with maximum specificity, so be sure to use these details in your grant proposal.[3]

This brings us to one of the most difficult aspects of writing grant proposals: how to demonstrate mastery of a large quantity of subject matter in a small space. One technique that is hard to pull off but almost never fails to impress readers: make a broad general statement about your subject, then support it with multiple examples from a diverse set of sources. Do so in a single paragraph consisting of sentences that are varied in length and complexity. Few use this technique more effectively than Janet Browne, the biographer of Charles Darwin. The following paragraph describes a turning point in Darwin's intellectual development:

> What Darwin did not recognize until considerably later was how far he was also capable of drawing free from his acknowledged sources. He had diverged from Henslow long ago over the nature of terrestrial flatworms in Brazil and was looking forward to confirming his own point of view. He diverged from Kotzebue and Earle after witnessing mission projects in action, and experienced a sea change of opinion about the nature of primitive mankind, finding close links between savage and civilized races which other authorities at home publicly rejected. He found the courage to disagree with the captain over slavery. He believed he had a fresh new understanding of the reproduction of corals and other marine invertebrates. He gradually dissociated himself from his father's plan that he should become a clergyman. He even diverged from Lyell in certain areas. He could improve on Lyell's theory of subterranean movements. He could demonstrate the steplike elevation of the Patagonian plains, the recent origins of parts of the Andes, the volcanic nature of the Galápagos Islands, and the formation of coral reefs. He could supplement much of what Lyell had to say about the geographical distribution of animals and plants and had some interesting theories about the extinction of fossil mammals to put before a scientific audience. Lyell, he thought, overestimated the way organisms were beautifully adapted to their surroundings.[4]

Here Browne makes a penetrating observation about Darwin's mind in the first sentence: he had achieved an intellectual maturity at this point in life that he recognized only later. Browne then lists the ways in which he demonstrated this independence. Her sentences are of varied length. But by beginning most of the sentences with the word "he," she makes it clear that what you are reading is, in essence, a list. Browne does not need to footnote each item in the list because she has already done so, extensively, over the preceding chapters, narrating Darwin's experience on the HMS *Beagle* as it circumnavigated the globe. But in your research narrative you can and should footnote such paragraphs. I recommend that you do so in a single note at the end of the paragraph, rather than in multiple notes in the body of it, since an overabundance of tiny superscript numbers would distract the reader and interrupt the flow of your writing.[5]

Ideas emerge from the accumulation of knowledge. Decisions on who should get grant money often turn on the amount of work the applicants have done to prepare themselves for focused research. This means you may have to struggle for quite a while to get research done with little or no financial support. Make no mistake: if you are at the beginning of your career as a researcher, you are at a disadvantage. But once you've been able to get some small amount of time carved out for research, and money to pursue it with, it gets easier. When, in the process of researching one topic, you stumble on another one that could be interesting, take note of it. You can develop it later and apply for research funding to look at it in depth. Thus money breeds more money, and grants beget grants. It is not exactly fair, but once you've made it into the favored group, you can make the system work for you.

Chapter 6

DIVE INTO THE SCHOLARSHIP

When I was in junior high school, there was a movie called *Faces of Death* that boys in my class spoke of with reverent horror and fascination. It was a kind of documentary with footage of people being killed, by execution, murder, wild animal attacks, suicide, and who knows what else. I'm happy to say I never saw it. But some years ago, I was witness to a similar spectacle at the annual conference of the American Historical Association. It happened when I joined members of my department in interviewing candidates for an assistant professorship. Most of the time, making decisions on the basis of these interviews is intensely difficult, because the interviewees are so polished and excellent. But in this case, a startling number of the candidates committed professional suicide before our eyes, thus making the committee's decisions about them painfully easy. They did so by failing to acknowledge the existence of scholarship related to their own, or by making claims to originality that were easily refuted.

It is a move that younger scholars often make that never fails to annoy more experienced ones. This kind of failed intellectual encounter is interesting in two ways. Why do younger scholars so often make this mistake? And why do older ones find it so annoying? Younger scholars often make the mistake of thinking that, if anyone else has written on their topic, it lacks novelty and hence value. The opposite is the case. The fact that others care about your topic enough to write about it means that it is important. More experienced scholars find the mistake grating partly for generational reasons. The people who render judgment on the work of younger scholars are generally older scholars, and when younger scholars fail to acknowledge that older ones have come before them and paved the way, the elders feel disrespected. A simpler explanation is that no one likes the combination of arrogance and ignorance. If you crow about having invented the wheel, and then try to get people to pay you royalties for it while the rest of the world is thinking about driverless cars and commercial space flight, you look like a dunce. So don't claim to have made earth-shattering discoveries when you haven't, and don't pretend you are the only person who ever written on topics related to yours. And even if you really are the first person ever to write on your topic, don't admit it. Disguise that fact by displaying your knowledge of scholarship on similar or contiguous topics. Your goal is to contribute to an ongoing conversation on topics that many people agree are important. It is not to diss the whole academy by saying you are the only person in history to recognize the epoch-making importance of your research.

One of the first obstacles grant seekers must overcome, then, is to master the secondary literature relevant to their research. This is more complicated than it sounds, since often there will be little to no scholarship on the exact topic you are working on. You will have to think carefully about what books and articles are relevant and should go into your reading pile. Which of these published works take interesting angles on similar topics? What topics are similar to yours? Who do you want to read your book? What do you want to change their minds about? You will have to prepare thoughtful answers to all these questions, and do the legwork that follows, if you want to avoid appearing on someone's academic *Faces of Death* highlight reel.

For instance, say you have identified a person whom you consider more important and fascinating than anyone ever has before, and you want to write a biography of that person. Perhaps there is a stray article or two on her, but no monographs or biographies. In one sense, this is a good thing: there is a gap in the literature that you can fill. But before you manufacture the scholarly brick that will fit into that gap in the Great Wall of Knowledge, you need to think about what bricks lie above, below, and beside the empty space you are eyeing. If you don't, the grant proposal evaluator may say that the reason nobody has written on your topic is that it is insignificant. By fleshing out the context, you can show that the gap really needs filling.

This is exactly the issue my colleague, Justin Castro, faces in writing the biography of Modesto Rolland. I had never heard of Rolland before Castro brought him to my attention. Rolland was a civil engineer who was prominent before, during, and after the Mexican Revolution. If Castro had provided me with only that information, I could have easily replied that this midlevel Mexican bureaucrat was not somebody whose biography interested me. But in the grant proposals he's written, Castro provides a great deal of contextual information to make it clear why I should be interested. He describes the ways in which Mexico is depicted in both scholarship and popular culture: it is often seen as a place of wild adventure, lawlessness, delicious food, lovely beaches, interesting native cultures, widespread poverty, and a complicated revolutionary history in which leftist insurrection led to modest gains in social welfare for ordinary people. Modesto Rolland complicates that vision. Rolland was a brilliant man of science, and his successes before the revolution demonstrate that the supposedly reactionary government of Porfirio Díaz was more sincerely committed to using science to promote social welfare than most people understand. Rolland's amazing continued success after the revolution, too, indicates that the revolutionary government was more committed to scientific progress than its pistol-shooting public image might lead one to believe. Castro shows that science and scientists have been deeply woven into the fabric of Mexican political culture since the eighteenth century, if not before. By mastering a huge amount of literature on Mexican history and culture, Castro has been able to convince others in his field that the life of this rather gray-seeming, midlevel engineer stands to reveal hidden worlds of Mexican scientific and political history. Not to mention that Castro has gained access to Rolland's never-before-seen personal papers and has discovered that Rolland was something of a closet sadist. Now that is a project that funding agencies can, and have, invested in.

Pick up any scholarly book on your shelf, and you will likely find a section of the introduction that tries to show the importance of the book's topic by referring to a body of scholarly literature. One of the historians who first inspired me to study history is the great China scholar Jonathan

D. Spence. Few historians handle secondary literature with as sure a hand as he does. In the preface to the second edition of his great narrative history *The Search for Modern China,* he writes that, since the book's first edition,

> Our knowledge of China's past has been prodigiously extended. Rich archaeological discoveries inside China are transforming our view of early Chinese society and the early texts on the theory of government. And also in countless areas closer to our current age, studies by Chinese and foreign scholars have profoundly altered what we thought we knew.
>
> In attempting to incorporate these findings into this second edition, I have been compelled to alter many old ideas, and to introduce many new ones. Prominent among these for the Qing dynasty itself would be the following: the ways that the eighteenth-century Manchu emperors of China transformed themselves into central Asian rulers; the stages by which secret societies came to play such a dominant role in challenging the state in China from the eighteenth century onward; the nature of women's literacy and education in the Qing, and the uses made of imagery of women in the loyalist politics of the time; the typologies of Chinese nationalism as they developed in the late Qing, and the impact of new forms of print media in circulating them widely.[1]

Here Spence offers a generous but efficient description of the ways in which recent scholarship has compelled him to change his views. Spence's authority is not diminished by admitting that some of his old ideas were wrong. It is enhanced. This is so because of the vast erudition Spence displays here, and because he adheres to the bedrock principle of intellectual life: one's mind must change when confronted with compelling new evidence.

Spence then goes on to discuss his critics:

> Some readers and reviewers of the first edition expressed a wish that the book had been organized along topical or conceptual lines, rather than on chronological ones, and that it had paid even more attention to broad social trends and the experiences of those completely divorced from the various political centers. They also sought more attention to various current Western theories, such as postmodernism,

subaltern studies, or various derivatives of those schools that claim
neo-Marxist credentials. On these points I remain unrepentant. Both
teachers and students of history need to know when things happened
before they begin to understand why. Of course the forces generated
within Chinese society affected the ideas and lives of the leaders,
or would-be leaders, just as did the might or the ideas imposed on
China by foreign powers. But I still feel that the attempt to make
sense of these varying impulses can most fittingly—in a historical
introduction of this kind—be undertaken from the center, looking
out. As to imposing stronger theoretical criteria for the selection or
organization of information, though this might be of interest to some
readers, it will puzzle or deter others; and given the nature of the
current Western cultural world, any theory chosen would in addition
be speedily outdated.[2]

For the moment, let's leave aside the content of Spence's response to his
critics, because both criticism and rebuttal are profound. What is key here
is that Spence makes no secret of the fact that people disagree with him.
He gives the critics their due, then sharpens his opposition to them, clari-
fying where and what those disagreements are. The power of Spence's response is intensified by his previous admission that some of his critics did
indeed persuade him. When you are doubtful about how best to handle
the secondary literature in your grant proposal, you might try taking a
book down from your shelf and see how masters like Spence do it.

Spence's approach to the delicate game of discussing his colleagues'
scholarship is certainly not the only viable one. Some of the very best
scholars have taken a more confrontational path, stating in essence that all
earlier writers on their topics are idiots. J. H. Hexter, celebrated historian
of seventeenth-century England, was famous for writing in this vein. In a
review of a collection of Hexter's essays, Quentin Skinner has collected
some of Hexter's choice putdowns. Hexter dismisses a historian's research
as "fairly extensive if desultory reading," and another's as "a rather hasty
look at the more obvious sources." Considering that these barbs are directed at Lawrence Stone and Christopher Hill, two of the most eminent
historians of the twentieth century, you can imagine what he says about
everyone else. Hexter can pull it off for a couple of reasons. One is that his
learning is expansive and his scholarship is precise. Another is that his

pugnacious treatment of other scholars contrasts pleasantly with his sensitive treatment of historical sources. Skinner's review ends on a very un-Hexterian note, generously arguing that, for all his spiky treatment of his peers, Hexter's contributions are valuable.[3]

I don't recommend that you put a Hexter on other people's scholarship. One reason is that scholarly progress can be made without trampling on others. If it is possible, then why not be kind? A second reason is that this kind of rhetoric can blow up in your face. You never know who is going to read your grant proposal, so why risk trashing someone, or someone's friend, or someone's mentor, who may have the power to deny your application? The scholarly world is a small one, and it gets smaller the more specialized your field. It is better to be respectful yet forthright, and so avoid poisoning the well you hope to drink from.

A final practical matter: if the grant application requires you to include a bibliography, you should spend a great deal of time crafting it. Far from being an afterthought or a decoration, the bibliography is often the first thing that evaluators look at. All evaluators have stories of bibliographies that were an ill-formatted mishmash of primary sources and outdated scholarship, and that made them want to say, "What the hell is this? Congratulations on not getting any grant money Mr. Applicant. You're a disgrace!" Don't be one of those applicants. Meticulously select a representative sample of the scholarship relevant to your topic. Cite the best scholarship, old and new, with a few thoughtfully chosen theoretical texts. Consult the *Chicago Manual of Style* to make sure you've formatted everything perfectly. If you know, or suspect you know, the identity of any member of the selection committee, make sure to cite his or her most relevant works. Constructing your bibliography can be a tedious exercise, but it is hugely important. Do not neglect it.

Chapter 7

KNOW YOUR THEORY

I once heard a horror story about an academic job talk in which a candidate gave a fascinating presentation on the history of education in Egypt. The department was seriously considering hiring the person who gave the talk. The talk was well-written, expertly delivered, and had many intriguing visual images to accompany it. But things started to go downhill in the question and answer period. Some people are better than others at thinking on their feet, and this person was not as adept at responding to questions as he was at presenting. The final nail in the coffin of his candidacy for the job came when someone asked how French officials' imperial education program related to the writings of Rousseau. It quickly became clear that the candidate had never read Rousseau. If he had, he would have known that the educational agenda of the French officials he was talking about was a thoroughly Rousseauist one. Needless to say, the candidate did not get the job.

There are many similar circumstances in which people conduct research, gather fascinating data, and do their best to analyze it without being fully aware of the theoretical principles that guide them, or that guide the people or phenomena they are studying. The historian John Womack offers a withering critique of new cultural historians, "who may or may not have read Rousseau or Kant or Nietzsche or Saussure or Lévi-Strauss or Derrida or Foucault, but who take the real-world past if not present too as a matter only of language." Whether or not Womack is right about the underlying issues, it does seem reasonable to expect that those who want to write Foucauldian histories will read Foucault's books.[1]

Theories of social structure are daunting, yet fertile, powerful, and above all, useful across many disciplines. They have the potential to connect empirical research to the interests of scholars working in multiple fields. Foucault, to take one obvious example, is cited in fields as disparate as the sociology of crime and punishment, the political analysis of rebellion and revolution, and the interpretation of Renaissance literary texts. Pierre Bourdieu's theory of "distinction" can be found in studies of the sociology of the family, of religious tolerance and intolerance, and of literary canon formation. One scholar recently made fascinating use of the anthropologist James C. Scott's *Domination and the Arts of Resistance* as a way of understanding Jane Austen's *Mansfield Park* and its oddly passive yet unexpectedly powerful protagonist. Whether you are turned on or turned off by the prospect of contemplating deep tomes of social theory, you should at the very least do some exploring in the theoretical literature that touches your field.[2]

For those who, regardless of their discipline, consider theory foreign territory, I recommend *History and Social Theory* by Peter Burke. Whatever field of the social sciences or humanities you work in, the book will probably be useful to you in its description of the uses of theory. Burke offers a wonderfully concise introduction to the various social theories that have influenced the practice of history, and the few historical studies that have produced novel theoretical approaches to understanding society. (If you're wondering what brilliant histories fall into the latter group, Burke cites Edward P. Thompson's study of "moral economy" and Eric Hobsbawm's work on "invented traditions.") Burke offers concise descriptions of the contribution and significance of the titans of the Western theoretical tradition from Plato and Aristotle, through Marx and Smith, and up to such ubiquitously cited twentieth-century gurus as Bourdieu, Foucault, and Fernand Braudel. In rereading this book, I felt a number of light bulbs, long dark, flickering to life in my head, as I realized how various theorists had influenced the way I think about documents, society, and history.[3]

Burke has a particularly valuable passage on the writings of the sixteenth-century British philosopher Francis Bacon:

In a famous passage, Francis Bacon formulated equally pungent criticisms of the antlike empiricists, who simply collected data, and of the pure theorists, spiders whose webs originated within themselves. Bacon recommended the example of the bee, who searches for raw material but also transforms it. His parable is as applicable to the history of historical and social research as it is to the history of the natural sciences. Without the combination of history and theory we are unlikely to understand either the past or the present.[4]

No matter what your field, my guess is that the vast majority of the readers of this book would do well to take Bacon and Burke's advice. Perhaps some humanists and social scientists will be spiders, focusing entirely on abstract theoretical questions, such as what the mathematical premises are for our understanding of macroeconomic policy, or how literary theorists responded to the publication of Noam Chomsky's theory of generative grammar. But pure theoreticians are not the majority. Nor will many applicants for research funding be pure empirical ants, given over entirely to the collection of data. Considering the broad influence of theory throughout the academy, none of these ants will get much funding. The vast majority of successful applicants are bees: that is, researchers who are industrious in both the collection of data out in the world, and in the transformation of that data through the creative application of ideas.

In your grant proposal, your discussion of theory should be economical and direct, acknowledging theoretical achievement while showing how your work either confirms, adds interesting detail to, or undermines it. Let us look at an example of unique relevance to this book. In *How Professors Think: Inside the Curious World of Academic Judgment*, Michèle Lamont offers the following description of the theories of sociologists Richard Whitley and Pierre Bourdieu that bear on her topic. Whitley, she writes, argues that disciplines that depend on the pooling of resources tend put scientists into competition with one another, and that the more pooling they require, the more competitive these disciplines are. In disciplines like English literature, scholarship is judged in subjective ways that rely on personal contacts. Bourdieu focuses on scientists struggling to impose their vision of excellence on the scholarly world. Both Whitley and Bourdieu say that scholars compete to define the criteria of excellence. But neither, says Lamont, offers an inductive analysis of those criteria. She then describes her own work:

In contrast, this book provides a detailed empirical analysis of the meaning of criteria on which scholars rely to distinguish "excellent" and "promising" research from less stellar work.

My approach differs from Bourdieu's in other ways. Bourdieu argues that the judgments of scholars reflect and serve their position in their academic field, even if they naturalize these judgments and legitimize them in universalistic terms. While he examines the social and economic filtering that lie behind interests, he does not consider whether and how defending excellence is central to the self-concept of many academics and how aspects of disinterestedness, such as pleasure, can be more than a self-serving illusion. In contrast, I factor into the analysis academics' sense of self and their emotions. While Bourdieu suggests that in the competition for distinction, conflicts are strongest among those occupying similar positions in fields, my interviews suggest that actors are motivated by not only the opportunity to maximize their position but also their pragmatic involvement in collective problem solving. Thus, contra Merton, Bourdieu, and Whitley, I oppose a view of peer review that is driven only or primarily by a competitive logic (or the market) and suggest in addition that peer review is an interactional and an emotional undertaking. In short, building on Goffman, my analysis suggests the importance of considering the self and emotions— in particular pleasure, saving face, and maintaining one's self-concept—as part of the investment that academics make in in scholarly evaluation.[5]

Lamont's book is an exceedingly sophisticated dive into the sociology of peer review, and those who want to know more should consult it, as well as the interview with her at the end of this book. But for our purposes, what is most relevant is that Lamont provides an elegant capsule description of the theorists whose ideas bear on the subject of her study. She then provides an equally elegant description of the ways her research reveals the inadequacies of those theories. She argues that Bourdieu in particular fails to understand the interplay of competition, emotion, and ideology that motivates peer reviewers. This represents two paragraphs out of a twenty-one-page introduction—about the same proportion you should dedicate to theory in your grant proposal.

Here is another example from a field closer to my own. *Chiricahua and Janos: Communities of Violence in the Southwestern Borderlands, 1680–1880,* by Lance Blyth, offers an admirably economical approach to discussing the theoretical ideas that guide him. He begins by telling the reader that Spanish settlers and Apache Indians did violence to one another for an astonishingly long time—two hundred years. "It is mind-boggling to think of a conflict running for that length of time," he writes. To make sense of this conflict, Blyth drew on work by David Nirenberg dealing with violence in the medieval world. Nirenberg's *Communities of Violence: Persecution of Minorities in the Middle Ages,*

provides the central insight of this work. Nirenberg looked at conflicts and violent episodes in the relations among Christians, Jews, Muslims, and lepers in northeastern Spain and southern France in the fourteenth and fifteenth centuries. He studied "cataclysmic" violence that featured attacks on Jews, lepers, and Muslims, motivated by rebellion against the monarchy and social conflict, and "systemic" violence, which arose from "everyday transgressions of religious boundaries" via conversion, interfaith sexuality, commensality, dress, and topography. As Nirenberg studied religious communities who were members of a single society and subjects of a medieval state, his categories and methods of analysis did not readily transplant to the Southwestern Borderlands. But his central thesis, that violence was no a sign of intolerance but was, instead, "a central and systematic aspect of the coexistence of majority and minorities in medieval Spain," and that "a constructive relationship between conflict and coexistence" prevailed, did cause me to rethink my assumptions about violence.

I took from Nirenberg the realization that violence is instrumental in establishing, maintaining, and changing relationships both within and between communities. Violence can be a useful tool for communities to employ, particularly in areas where no single political organization or cultural group has a monopoly on its use, such as borderlands. It is just such communities to which I apply Nirenberg's appellation of "communities of violence." While I focus on a borderland called the Southwestern Borderlands in expectation that most readers will view the region from this geographical viewpoint, there are many other borderlands at other times and other places.

Even a cursory study of those borderlands will likely reveal their own communities of violence.[6]

Here, as with Lamont, the scholar engages theory in a thoughtful way and shows how his subject matter sheds light on it. In both cases, theories provide as much guidance when they are wrong as when they are right. Showing how theories break down allows scholars to find new patterns in the evidence.

The practical implication of this is that some portion of your grant application should focus on the big ideas that guide your thinking about what you study. The amount of text in this section should probably be smaller than that focusing on scholarly literature, and certainly smaller than that focused on your research. But it should be in there somewhere, as a way of signaling to your readers that you are conscious of the ideas that have shaped your project. It should also show that you are sensitive both to the ways those ideas can help us understand what you study, and to the ways your research may force readers to question and challenge the reigning theories in your field.

Among the many advantages of engaging with theory is that you will make your work appealing to those who work on other things. They may not know much about the cases of social ostracism in the Sicilian countryside that fascinate you. But they may well have seen similar phenomena in the highlands of Burma, and may know of theoretical literature bearing on it that could be of use to you. Though it can be dauntingly abstract, theoretical literature can build bridges between you, your colleagues, and your evaluators. For this reason, I always try to include participants from multiple disciplines in grant-writing workshops. An economist who specializes in theories of irrational decision-making can help experts in the depiction of madness in Victorian literature. Art historians who know about patronage in eighteenth-century France can guide anthropologists working on inequality in South Asia to theoretical literature that sheds light on both topics. When assembling your own team of supporters, be sure to reach out to people who work on related topics in other disciplines so they can help you find common intellectual ground.

Just as there are benefits to engaging with theory, there are dangers to not doing so. I've sometimes seen younger scholars adopting the tone and rhetoric of curmudgeonly older ones and showering scorn on new-fangled theories. I've cited a couple of brilliant senior scholars who do just this—Jonathan Spence and John Womack. But I don't think it's a good idea for you to imitate them on this score. The Spences and Womacks of the world can afford to take contrarian positions because they stand no chance of being professionally hurt by doing so. They are senior scholars whose reputations are secure. It is also almost inevitable that people in the sunset—the brilliant, wonderfully impressive sunset!—of their careers will lament the disastrous paths down which the younger generations are leading the academy. That's just the way of the world. But when younger scholars trash new ideas, it strikes a jarring note, suggesting closed-mindedness and resentment. For most people, theory is foreign territory. As philosopher Robert Nozick puts it, "We all are immigrants to the world of thought." And as immigrants, it is wise at least to feign respect for the odd and sometimes distasteful customs of this foreign land. Beyond that, you never know who is going to read your application. Being resentfully angry about new ideas is more likely to alienate a reader than being curious and open-minded about them. I can't remember seeing someone go far in academia by saying, "Dammit, I'm just going to plow through a mountain of data, think about it real hard, and write it up like they did in the good old days, because I don't need pretentious *theories*." People do say things like that. But even if that's what you think, you probably should keep it to yourself. Beyond the question of appearances, it is also wise to keep an open mind to theoretical ideas that may help you see patterns you didn't realize were there.[7]

A related mistake I've seen is when people think that dropping a few names will act like fairy dust, adding a sparkle of novelty and sophistication to their work. People sometimes forget that Foucault died more than thirty years ago; his ideas cannot be accurately described as "new." I've seen a job talk in which a candidate tried to pass off economic dependency theories developed in the 1960s as if they were the latest thing. He convinced no one. Pay attention to what's going on in your field now, and try to gauge where the most relevant theorizing is going on. Engage with it honestly and don't expect it to do work for you that it can't do.

Chapter 8

IDENTIFY GRANT MAKERS

The Internet has made grant research easy. Simply go to Google, type in "research funding in the humanities and social sciences," and voilà! You will find a long list of grants you can apply for. You should also ask your recommenders where research money can be found. Ask peers and friends. Ask your department chair. Read the acknowledgments of books in your field and see who funded the research behind them. Research universities tend to have offices that help faculty find and manage grant money. Among the major institutions to look at are the

American Academy in Berlin
American Antiquarian Society
American Association of University Women
American Council of Learned Societies
American Philosophical Society
Ford Foundation
Harry Frank Guggenheim Foundation
Horowitz Foundation for Social Policy
John Simon Guggenheim Foundation
Library of Congress

Mellon Foundation
National Endowment for the Arts
National Endowment for the Humanities
National Science Foundation
Newberry Library
Rockefeller Foundation
Russell Sage Foundation
Social Science Research Council
U.S. Department of Defense
U.S. Department of State
Wenner-Gren Foundation

Beyond these, your university, department, or academic unit may have research money you can apply for. Also, libraries and archives often have small grants for people who want to visit them. Simply go to the website of each of these institutions and search for grants you are eligible for. Make a list of about a dozen, and prioritize those grants and fellowships for which your project seems like the best fit. Put the deadlines on your calendar and plan to submit your application a week or two early.

When I've run my grant-application workshop, I have created an online Google Calendar that all participants have access to. My first assignment is for each participant to go online and locate ten grants they would like to apply for, and to put the application deadlines on the calendar, along with a description of the grant. No grant can be listed twice. Thus the participants who get the assignment done first, listing the better-known grants and fellowships, force the stragglers to search further afield. The collective result is a very thorough job of grant research. Everyone has access to all the information on the calendar. From the first moment, it is clear that all such information has to be shared, and that no one in the group will try to profit from anyone else's ignorance. Everyone is helping everyone else. Those who fail to complete this assignment are barred from continuing the workshop.

Chapter 9

LOCK DOWN THOSE CRITERIA

It is hard to overstate how important it is to study the criteria of evaluation for each of the grant competitions you enter. Let's see if I can overstate it: failing to study those criteria is worse than shooting a photon torpedo through the crater of Vesuvius, into the Earth's core, and blowing the planet into galactic nothingness. I did it! I overstated its importance. Not studying the criteria for grant competitions is not that bad. But it's close.

The criteria for the Fulbright-Hays grant are particularly intricate, and so present a sort of worst-case scenario. If you are prepared for this, you'll be prepared for pretty much anything. Fulbright-Hays breaks down its selection criteria into a variety of categories, in which a certain number of points can be won. Here are the program's priorities. Prepare yourself for a horrendous pile of tedious verbiage:

a. **Absolute**: The Department will only consider applications that meet this priority. This priority is: A research project that focuses on one or more of the following geographic areas: Africa, East Asia, Southeast Asia and the Pacific Islands, South Asia, the Near East, Central and Eastern Europe and Eurasia, and the Western Hemisphere (excluding the United States and its territories). Please note that applications that propose projects focused on the following countries are not eligible: Andorra, Austria, . . . [etc.]

b. **Competitive Preference Priority 1 (3 points)**: A research project that focuses on one or more of the following geographic areas: Sub-Saharan Africa: Angola, Benin, Botswana, Burkina Faso, . . . [etc.]

c. **Competitive Preference Priority 2 (2 points):** A research project that focuses on any of the seventy-eight (78) languages selected from the U.S. Department of Education's list of Less Commonly Taught Languages (LCTLs) as follows: Akan (Twi-Fante), Albanian, Amharic, . . . [and seventy-five more]

d. **Competitive Preference Priority 3 (5 points):** A research project in the field of economics, engineering, international development, global education, mathematics, political science, public health, science, or technology proposed by an applicant who will use advanced language proficiency in one of the 78 LCTLs listed in Competitive Preference Priority 2 of this notice in his or her research. An applicant must meet all three components of this priority in order to be awarded points: propose a research project in one of the fields listed above, be proficient in the language of research at an advanced level, and propose using as a language of research one of the 78 LCTLs listed in this notice.

e. **Invitational Priority:** While no additional points will be awarded to an application that meets this priority, we encourage applications from Minority-Serving Institutions. . . . [etc.]

That is a steaming heap of verbosity if ever there was one! What does it all mean? It means, first, that the government will fund projects for some countries and not for others. Make sure your country is not on the ineligible list. Second, the government wants people to study certain less-often-taught languages. If you know and plan to use one of these languages in your research, make sure you mention it, because you will get extra points in the competition. Third, the government favors science and social science over the humanities. If you are in a favored discipline, make sure you put that in. If you are in a disfavored one, but use methods from a favored one, mention that. It may be worth a point or two, and every point counts. Also, if you are a minority, or study at a Minority Serving Institution, say so in your application. It could break ties in your favor.

Let's move on to the selection criteria. Hold your breath and prepare for a deep dive into the murky depths of more government-issue excess. The selection criteria for the evaluation of each project are assigned numerical values as follows:

(1) The statement of the major hypotheses to be tested or questions to be examined, and the description and justification of the research methods to be used (15 points);
(2) The relationship of the research to the literature on the topic and to major theoretical issues in the field, and the project's originality and importance in terms of the concerns of the discipline (10 points);
(3) The preliminary research already completed in the United States and overseas or plans for such research prior to going overseas, and the kinds, quality, and availability of data for the research in the host country or countries (10 points);
(4) The justification for overseas field research and preparations to establish appropriate and sufficient research contacts and affiliations abroad (10 points);
(5) The applicant's plans to share the results of the research in progress and a copy of the dissertation with scholars and officials of the host country or countries (5 points); and
(6) The guidance and supervision of the dissertation advisor or committee at all stages of the project, including guidance in developing the project, understanding research conditions abroad, and acquainting the applicant with research in the field (10 points).

The program also considers the qualifications of each applicant, which it breaks down thus:

(1) The overall strength of the applicant's graduate academic record (10 points);
(2) The extent to which the applicant's academic record demonstrates strength in area studies relevant to the proposed project (10 points);
(3) The applicant's proficiency in one or more of the languages (other than English and the applicant's native language) of the country or countries of research, and the specific measures to be taken to overcome any anticipated language barriers (15 points); and

(4) The applicant's ability to conduct research in a foreign cultural context, as evidenced by the applicant's references or previous overseas experience, or both (5 points).

This wordiness is both good news and bad news for you. The bad news is that it is a chore to slog through. The good news is that many foolish applicants won't do the work of slogging, and so may forfeit points through laziness and imprecision. You won't, though. So the verbiage presents a potential opportunity.

What does this all mean? Make sure you explicitly state your hypothesis and describe and justify your research methods. Be sure to show how your project relates to your field. Demonstrate that you have done superb preliminary research, and that you know precisely which sources you will examine while abroad. Item (4), worth a juicy ten points, is easily overlooked: show that you have contacts in the country you want to visit. Making these contacts can be as simple as sending an email to a scholar overseas, or asking an adviser or colleague to help with introductions. Just thirty seconds of work could earn you ten points. Sweet! Amazingly, many will fail to do this, and so won't get the loot. The same is true for the foreign language section: get a letter from a language teacher certifying that you know the language you'll be working in. Ten minutes of work for no fewer than fifteen points. Don't mess this up.

About the dissertation adviser section: make sure your adviser knows about this. Copy it and send it to him in an email, and make sure he responds to every facet of the requirement in his letter of recommendation. The same advice goes for the "Qualifications" section. Write with great specificity about your own experience, and answer each question in concrete detail. Some people may delude themselves into thinking the grant is mainly for people who have never before traveled abroad. To quote Fox News anchor Megyn Kelly: "Wrong, Sir, *wrong!*" It says in item four of the qualifications section that previous overseas travel is positive, to the tune of five huge points. So go ahead, mention the trip to Tijuana you took with your parents when you were eleven. If that's all the experience you've got, it could still be worth a point or two.

My selection of the Fulbright-Hays criteria stems from a painful experience. After I applied and was rejected, I asked to see the comments of the readers. The readers' reports said the project was great, but that the total absence of support from my advisers had torpedoed me. When I showed this to my advisers, they were furious. They had sent their recommendations weeks ahead of time, but the letters somehow got lost in the Fulbright-Hays computer system. I applied again the next year and got the grant. Here's another reason I use these criteria: a friend of mine was also rejected, asked for her readers' reports, and discovered that she had failed by the narrowest of margins. The reason she failed was that she had forfeited ten points by failing to show that she had professional contacts in the host country. After overcoming her rage at this injustice, she too applied again the following year and got it. Both of us received grants of between forty-five and fifty thousand dollars. Small mistakes can cost you, big time. Don't make them.

Part III

PROCESS

Chapter 10

PREPARATION STRATEGIES: AN OVERVIEW

After reading this far, some of you may realize you are not ready to apply for grant money. There's no shame in that discovery. Most people aren't, since before you can be ready you have to acquire all the skills and materials described in Chapters 4 through 9. If doing that means finishing coursework for your master's or your Ph.D. orals reading, by all means do so. Reading the first parts of this book may have provided you with a clearer idea of why those tasks are important. So if you haven't done so already, focus on getting the knowledge and the network of supporters you need, the better to compete for grant funding in the future.

If you've secured 80 percent of what has been described in earlier chapters—a research question, subject matter, knowledge of the relevant scholarship and theory, a list of grants to apply for, and the criteria by which the competitions are judged—you should continue. Even if you've locked down only 50 percent of it, you should continue. Continuing will help you get all those materials collected.

You will need a writing group, a place to meet, and, if you like, a leader or coordinator to address practical matters. Once you've got all that lined up, proceed to Chapter 11 and start working on your outline.

Chapter 11

GENERATE AN OUTLINE

I once read a description of the philosopher Robert Nozick that reminded me of NHL legend Wayne Gretzky. The writer described Nozick's philosophy as at once "rigorous" and "playful." Those two words brought Gretzky to mind: his joyful creativity and his fierce focus on technique. Everything he did was wildly unexpected, yet it was always executed with amazing precision. Rigor combined with playfulness: it is as good a capsule description of virtuosity as I've ever read. Mozart has the same quality. His piano concertos always seem to me as precise as a perfectly cut diamond, yet as playful as a baby monkey. Perhaps none of us can aspire to such transcendent excellence, though we can aspire to join rigor and playfulness in our own work. But how? The two qualities seem to conflict with one another. Precise and meticulous people often lack the spark of playfulness, while playfully unpredictable minds are often everything but precise.'

I came across a wonderful guide to the yoking of playfulness and rigor—the baby monkey of creativity with the plodding gem-cutter of precision—in a book called *Making Your Case: The Art of Persuading Judges* by Antonin Scalia and Brian Garner. Yes, that Antonin Scalia. Whatever you may think of his jurisprudence, Justice Scalia is by all accounts one of the very best writers ever to sit on the Supreme Court. Garner and Scalia's focus is on how to produce maximally persuasive legal briefs at high speed and under extreme pressure. They draw on a technique developed by University of Texas writing instructor Betty Sue Flowers called "Madman, Architect, Carpenter, Judge." The idea is simple and powerful. It is to split the process of writing into four distinct and mutually inimical stages, with no stage overlapping with any of the others.[2]

In the first stage, which Flowers calls "Madman," you work at furious speed generating as many ideas as possible, listing whatever occurs to you with minimal regard for relevance, precision, or polish. The idea is to let ideas flow, without the impediment of self-criticism. The absence of self-consciousness makes it possible to air ideas that may seem silly at first, but that might well turn out to be serious on closer examination. There is a wonderful exchange in Boswell's *Life of Johnson* that this brings to my mind. In discussing the ethics of lawyering, Boswell poses a question:

> BOSWELL: But what do you think of supporting a cause which you know to be bad?
> JOHNSON: Sir, you do not know it to be good or bad until the judge determines it. I have said that you are to state facts fairly; so that your thinking, or what you call knowing, a cause to be bad, must be from reasoning, must be from your supposing your arguments to be weak and inconclusive. But, Sir, that is not enough. An argument which does not convince yourself, may convince the Judge to which you urge it; and if it does convince him, why, then, Sir, you are wrong and he is right. It is his business to judge; and you are not to be confident in your own opinion that a cause is bad, but to say all you can for your client, and then hear the Judge's opinion.[3]

In the early stages, as you think about your own writing, you should imitate the good lawyer described by Johnson. Do not presume to know which of your ideas is good and which is bad. You will judge that later. For now, just let ideas flow.

Once the flow of ideas slackens, after perhaps a half-hour of brainstorming, bring the "Madman" phase to a close. Garner and Scalia urge you to put your notes aside for an hour and give your mind a rest. Thereafter, go back to your notes, comb through them, and think about which of your ideas is strongest, which is weakest, and how you should put them in order. This phase, "Architect," is where you make a simple outline, listing your ideas and the evidence that supports them. Give your mind a rest once you're done, then move on to phase three.

Phase three, "Carpenter," is where you draft your brief, working hard to bring it into existence as quickly as you can, with little regard for polish. Screw-ups, splinters, and rough edges are fine here. This is the hardest part of the whole process. The key is to create a draft that will give you something to work with and reshape. Remember this: all first drafts are perfect. Why? Because their only task is to exist. At the conclusion of this phase, take a rest once again.

"Judge" is the enemy of "Madman." Where the madman is sloppy and creative, the judge is meticulous and critical. It is in this phase that one sands down rough edges, eliminates everything that is stupid or worthless, and buffs the final product up to a high gloss. The focus here is on precision and polish, dotting i's and crossing t's. Did you properly italicize that comma? Are your footnotes exquisitely pedicured? Did you remember to include a strong title? Make sure you can answer all these questions in the affirmative. And then you're done. At least with your first full draft.

The beauty of this process is that it gives ample scope to both crazy creativity and sober self-critique. Garner and Scalia pinpoint a serious problem for many writers, which is that they allow their critical faculties to stymie their creative ones. By failing to brainstorm freely enough, or by interrupting their brainstorms with the stern voice of reason, many writers never allow themselves the freedom to do original work. The opposite problem is equally common. By never judging one's own ideas critically, many writers permit others to do so for them. Thus they allow good but underdeveloped thoughts to be crushed before they can spread their wings and fly.

At its best, the Flowers/Garner/Scalia method allows writers to give their entire minds broad scope for action. Creativity works in tandem with critical analysis, rather than against it. Critical analysis is kept from stamping out the spark of inspiration. The baby monkey learns to balance a ball on its nose. Bartleby the Scrivener learns to tango.

What you should do in this phase of your grant-proposal-writing process is akin to the "Madman" and "Architect" phases. Brainstorm a list of the ideas, secondary literature, and evidence that you think may end up in the final product. Once you have one single-spaced page filled, take a breather. Come back in about an hour or so and move the most important ideas to the top of the list, followed by the most important evidence and secondary literature on topics contiguous to yours. Don't overthink this, and whatever you do, do not aim for perfection or comprehensiveness. Doing so will do damage to both the process and the product. You need an outline that can be reshaped and reordered without much difficulty.

It is important to be able to jettison old ideas and adopt new ones without much effort once you meet with your writing group. What often happens is your peers will tell you that what you thought is your most important point is actually less important than secondary or supporting points. They may say something like, "Your main argument is so strong that, in fact, you don't need to argue it. Everyone already agrees with it. What is more interesting to me is how you arrive at that argument. You use X piece of evidence in ways no one else has." Or they may say, "This is a fabulous argument, but I don't think there is evidence out there that can possibly prove it. Why not reframe the question in this way?" Or: "The evidence you've got is incredibly interesting and novel, but I don't think the argument you are spinning out of it does justice to the innovativeness of the research you've done." The key thing is to get your project to a place where you can absorb creative suggestions like these without too much work. If the project is totally "cooked," you won't be able to add new ingredients without restarting from scratch.

Chapter 12

CREATE A FIRST DRAFT

Let's pretend for a moment that your proposal is a Thanksgiving dinner and members of the grant-making committee are your guests. And let's say that instead of sources and scholarly literature, the ingredients you need for your grant are turkey, carrots, fingerling potatoes, sweet potatoes, broccoli rabe, parmesan cheese, salt, pepper, rosemary, butter, and olive oil. How shall you prepare these ingredients? In what order will you prepare them? In what combinations? How long will each element cook? Will you go to the corner store for spices? If so, which ones?

If you're short on time, one option is to throw all the ingredients into the Vitamix, flip the "on" switch, and serve the resulting mush to your guests as a smoothie. There may be worse solutions to the problem of cooking for large numbers of people at the last minute. But I assure you, your guests have been served this particular meal many times, and they have come to expect a more thoughtful preparation.

There are better ways—many better ways—to prepare this dinner. Some have Chinese or Mexican touches. Some are light and elegant. Others are buttery and rich. There are cookbooks to consult, and tips that your friends and relations have passed down by word of mouth. But there is a common element to all successful Thanksgiving dinner plans: time enough to gather information and to plan the dinner, and a good long time set aside for the cooking itself. My recipe is below. You should use it as a mere starting point, adding your own style, spice, culture, and personal taste.

Switching back from metaphor to reality, your grant proposal should be roughly 2,500 words long, with proper *Chicago Manual of Style* footnotes and a two-page bibliography. Some grants ask for a longer narrative, others require a shorter one. A 2,500-word version will be relatively easy to scale up or down.

OPEN WITH A COMPELLING STORY

First, present a gripping short narrative from the research you have already completed. This narrative should both capture the reader's attention and call into doubt an important set of ideas from the secondary literature. A good example: the first two paragraphs of Susan Sheehan's Pulitzer Prize–winning book *Is There No Place on Earth for Me?*

> Shortly after midnight on Friday, June 16, 1978, Sylvia Frumkin decided to take a bath. Miss Frumkin, a heavy, ungainly young woman who lived in a two-story yellow brick building in Queens Village, New York, walked from her bedroom on the second floor to the bathroom next door and filled the tub with warm water. A few days earlier, she had had her hair cut and shaped in a bowl style, which she found especially becoming, and her spirits were high. She washed her brown hair with shampoo and also with red mouthwash. Some years earlier, she had tinted her hair red and had liked the way it looked. She had given up wearing her hair red only because she had found coloring it every six weeks too much of a bother. She imagined that the red mouthwash would somehow be absorbed into her scalp and make her hair red permanently. Miss Frumkin felt so cheerful about her new haircut that she suddenly thought she was Lori Lemaris, the mermaid whom Clark Kent had met in college and had fallen in love with in the old "Superman" comics. She blew bubbles into the water.[1]

Sheehan goes on to tell the reader that Frumkin slipped while getting out of the bath, cut her head and ended up in the emergency room. But not before she had poured an expensive bottle of perfume on her head, partly because she knew it contained alcohol, and "partly because she suddenly

thought that she was Jesus Christ and that her bleeding cut was the beginning of a crown of thorns."[2]

Let's leave aside for a moment the fact that you probably won't be able
to spend two whole paragraphs on your opening narrative. This narrative
is absolutely fascinating on a number of levels. It has a Magritte-like quality of mingling the ordinary and the bizarre. It is both goofy and tragic. It
raises many questions: Red mouthwash? What? Why? How did this woman
come to be this way? How will she survive? Why do I care so much about
her? By what magic is Sheehan able to arrange simple words on the page
in such a way that the story suddenly blazes to life at the word "bath"?
What is going to happen? What does it all mean? Oh my God! It's amazing! It's unbelievable! So much so, in fact, that I am going to stop writing
this book right now and start reading *Is There No Place on Earth for Me?*

. . . Okay, I've finished reading it. And you know what? Those opening
two paragraphs I just quoted? They are the *least* interesting thing about the
book. I cried over poor Sylvia Frumkin's story, but I also shed tears of joy
over the author's consummate artistry in telling it. And I learned a great
deal about the mental health system in the United States. That is what I
mean when I write that you should begin your proposal with a gripping
and vivid opening narrative. Just make it one paragraph, not two.

Here's another example, taken from political scientist Moisés Naím's
Illicit: How Smugglers, Traffickers, and Copycats Are Hijacking the Global Economy. This is
the book's first paragraph:

> The famous former United States president, for eight years the most
> powerful man on earth, was born in a small country town blessed
> with "very good feng shui." As an adolescent struggling to excel in
> spite of his modest rural circumstances, he "admired the ambition of
> Gu Yanwu, who said we should walk 10,000 miles and read 10,000
> books." Often during his political career he sought wisdom and
> guidance from the sayings of Chairman Mao. As for the starstruck
> young intern with whom he had an affair that nearly destroyed his
> presidency, he had this to say: "She was very fat."[3]

Naím goes on to argue that the pirated edition of Bill Clinton's autobiog-
raphy quoted here, which came out months before the official Chinese
translation, typifies a massive problem in the world economy: that of

piracy of all kinds. He discusses pirated books, DVD's, and software; bogus prescription medications that can kill; and more sinister commodities, including narcotics, human kidneys, sex slaves, anthrax, and nuclear centrifuges. The introductory paragraph is a brilliant entrée into this dark world. It first causes a certain cognitive dissonance, inviting the reader to try to identify this curiously Chinese-sounding ex-president. It then gets stranger and stranger, funnier and funnier. And it culminates with an exquisitely stupid invented quotation.

Your opening paragraph is overwhelmingly important. Few grant-proposal readers will admit to this, but I guarantee you that many of them stop reading, or stop reading closely, if the first paragraph of a proposal stinks. Make sure your first paragraph provokes, amuses, and whets the intellectual appetites of your reader.

EXPLAIN HOW YOUR WORK WILL RESPOND TO A BODY OF SCHOLARSHIP

Second, tell the reader how the secondary and theoretical literature fails to help us understand the short story you've just told. This is where you demonstrate, with great efficiency, your command of the scholarly literature on your topic. In Sheehan's case, though she is writing an extended piece of narrative journalism and not a scholarly monograph, she nevertheless shows how both scholarly literature and mental health institutions have failed people like Sylvia Frumkin, despite earnest efforts to help them.

Here is another example. In Brian DeLay's multiple-award-winning study *War of a Thousand Deserts: Indian Raids and the U.S.-Mexican War,* the author first describes the signing of the Treaty of Guadalupe Hidalgo. He then describes his discovery of the treaty's eleventh article, which obligated the United States to prevent "savage Indians" from attacking Mexico. It also prohibited the purchase, by American citizens, of any Mexican citizens held captive by those Indians. That's right: a provision of the treaty told Americans, "Don't buy Mexican slaves from the savages." DeLay then writes:

> This all struck me as curious and fascinating. As someone interested in both nation-states and native peoples, I immediately wanted to learn more about the international alarms over Indians. Yet making sense of article 11 turned out to be harder than I expected. Over the past generation historians have done a great deal of work recovering the

roles native peoples played in inter-imperial conflicts in eastern
north America. Sometimes native peoples influenced these conflicts
directly, by lending military support to particular European powers.
But one of the chief virtues of the groundbreaking recent work on
this subject has been an insistence that Indian polities could just as
often influence imperial designs and colonial realities indirectly, by
pursuing independently their own complicated and shifting agendas.
Over the course of the eighteenth century, however, the geopolitical
significance of North America's autonomous Indians supposedly wore
away, peaking with the Seven Years' War, declining with the American
Revolution, and all but disappearing after the War of 1812. Thus
historians in the United States who have written about westward
expansion, Manifest Destiny, and the U.S. Mexican War have ignored
Indian raids in northern Mexico and say almost nothing about the
native peoples that so preoccupied the architects of article 11. Indians
are more visible in Mexican than in U.S. history, by a matter of
demographic necessity. Indigenous peasants are increasingly
prominent, for example, in the literature on early nineteenth century
Mexico. But the tens of thousands of independent Indians who
controlled the vast northern borderlands region rarely make it into
books about Mexico's early national period or into Mexican
scholarship on the War with the United States.[4]

Here DeLay offers a concise description of the rich literature on native peoples in eighteenth- and nineteenth-century North America, then identifies a
significant gap in it. Over the course of the book, he proceeds, brilliantly, to
fill that gap. Throughout, he keeps the secondary literature in view, but con-
centrates on explaining his own thorough and fascinating research.

Here is another example taken from Louise Walker's groundbreaking
study of the middle classes in post-revolutionary Mexico. Walker begins by
arguing that an analysis of the middle classes can transform our understanding of the Mexican state in the twentieth century. Yet few scholars have
done so, a failure that Walker explains in part by alluding to the Mexican's
government's desire to represent itself as the embodiment of the dreams of
a peasant revolution. Historians have in large measure followed the government's lead, and so have neglected middle-income Mexicans. "The lack of
attention to the middle classes," she writes,

might also reflect the scholars who have analyzed postrevolutionary Mexican history and society. Considering a similar lacuna in historical scholarship on the United States, one historian argues that it is related to a discomfort on the left, and especially leftist academics, with the category "middle class." Many scholars explicitly describe their work as a political project. Middle-class fears and insecurities do not fit well with a romantic, revolutionary narrative of political change. Many politically motivated scholars who analyze social movements, among other topics, have become invested in these narratives and consequently focus on the poor and marginalized as vehicles of social change from below.

No doubt, the middle classes appear in many studies as artisans, merchants, professionals, bureaucrats, teachers, Catholic activists, students, and countercultural aficionados. Few works, though, explicitly address questions of middle-class formation, politics, or cultures in Mexico. Often historians use the term "middle-class" as a descriptive adjective rather than a historically contingent category requiring analytical engagement. Indeed some scholars perform strenuous contortions to *not see* the middle-class status of those they study. Theorist Immanuel Wallerstein argues that the middle classes tend to function as a deus ex machina: like the literary device that suddenly—and inexplicably and unsatisfactorily—resolves the plot, they are reified, unexamined, and mystified. Whatever the reason, the politics of writing about the middle classes have shaped the scholarship on modern Mexico, in which the middle classes are conspicuous by their absence.[5]

In many ways this is a model of how to deal with the classic "gap in the literature" problem. Walker does not claim that the absence of scholarship on the middle classes is reason enough to study them. Rather, she draws on scholarship from contiguous fields—U.S. history and Wallerstein's "world systems" theories—to show that the scholars' failure to attend to the middle classes is itself a kind of analytical problem that she will address over the course of the book. Walker draws on an extremely thorough knowledge of the historiography and theoretical literature dealing with contiguous topics to show that her topic is both misunderstood and capable of revealing an enormous amount about the structure of Mexican social, political, and economic life in the late twentieth century.

Grant writers must do something similar but subtly different. Rather than describing what they *have* learned at book length, they must describe what they will learn over the course of about five carefully structured pages. But they must always have a passage near the beginning of the proposal that, like the ones shown earlier, demonstrates mastery of the secondary and theoretical literature.

TRANSITION TO YOUR RESEARCH QUESTION

Third, write something like this—but in your own words: "If we cannot make sense of the story I've just told using what we already know, the question becomes X." Then lay your one-sentence research question on the reader.

Here is how DeLay does it. He writes that violence has been a major theme in borderlands scholarship.

> But three gaps in this work, having to do with place, period, and connections, left me still puzzled that relations between native peoples and northern Mexicans would have been of such concern in Mexico City and Washington.[6]

Put in slightly different terms, why did the signers of the treaty of Guadalupe Hidalgo care about Indians and Mexicans in Mexico's northern provinces?

Here is another example. In *Quest for Equality: The Failed Promise of Black-Brown Solidarity*, Neil Foley begins by recounting a truly cringe-worthy gaffe made by Mexico's president Vicente Fox. Speaking to a group of Texas businessmen in 2005, Fox said, "There is no doubt that Mexicans, filled with dignity, willingness and ability to work, are doing jobs that not even blacks want to do in the United States." Oops. The implication that blacks (1) did only menial labor, and (2) were not as hardworking as Latinos, caused a first-class international kerfuffle. Then Foley writes:

> Whatever his intentions, Fox's racially fraught comment raised questions about the way Mexicans in general view black Americans, not to mention their own citizens of African descent.[7]

In other words: What are Mexicans' attitudes toward peoples of African descent? What do black people in the United States and Mexico think of people of Mexican origins? And what effects do these attitudes have on politics in the two countries? Interesting questions indeed.

ANSWER YOUR RESEARCH QUESTION

Offer a thesis that answers the research question you've posed. Take note: at this point, you should be no more than 15 to 20 percent of the way into your proposal. You should not make the reader wait any longer than that to find out your brilliant answer to the big question. Answering your research question early in the proposal does not ruin the suspense. It prepares the reader for what is to come. Remember *Romeo and Juliet*: the prologue gives away the ending.

> From forth the fatal loins of these two foes
> A pair of star-cross'd lovers take their life;
> Whose misadventured piteous overthrows
> Do with their death bury their parents' strife.[8]

God, that's wonderful. Now I want to go read it. But my point is that despite the prologue's giveaway, the play's final act is still surprising and tragic, because the drama is so well developed. Let your readers know early on what to expect, then blow their minds with your fascinating narrative.

Let's see how the pros do it. The answer to DeLay's research question—the statement of the book's argument—comes on the third page of the introduction to his more-than-four-hundred-page book:

> I argue that the bloody interethnic violence that preceded and
> continued throughout the U.S.-Mexican War influenced the course
> and outcome of that war and, by extension, helped precipitate its
> manifold long-term consequences for all the continent's peoples.[9]

Foley's answer comes on page nineteen of his book, which runs longer than two hundred pages:

> The history of African American and Mexican American civil rights
> activism in Texas and California during and after World War II reveals,
> more than anything, the missed opportunities and the failed promise

of these groups to work together for economic rights and equal
education.[10]

Here's another example. On the third page of the introduction to Martin
Luther: The Christian between God and Death, Richard Marius writes:

> As Luther confessed time and again, his was a temperament driven
> by fear and by the need to conquer it so he could live day by day. His
> greatest terror, one that came on him periodically as a horror of
> darkness, was the fear of death—death itself, not the terror of a
> burning and eternal hell awaiting the sinner in an afterlife.[11]

Interestingly, most historians think Marius is wrong about this. Luther
probably did believe in the afterlife, and was not afraid his soul would dis-
solve into nothingness after he died. But because Marius states his case
early, because he does so with such conviction, and because he sustains the
thesis throughout the book with such fierce brilliance, one comes away
from it stimulated to thought, if not persuaded by the argument.

State your argument early in your proposal and support it as vigor-
ously as you can. Take risks and don't be afraid to be wrong. If you change
your mind in the process of writing, that is normal. But in the proposal,
state forcefully what you think right now.

GO DEEPER, EXPLAIN IN MORE DETAIL

In the body of the proposal, offer a deeper dive into your research to date,
showing in detail both the work you have completed so far and the work
that remains to be done. One effective way of structuring this section is by
chapters: giving a section-by-section outline of the book/dissertation/
article you plan to write lets the reader know you are thinking strategically. This is where you demonstrate that you will complete an ambitious
research program in a reasonable period of time. You will make it obvious
to the reader that you have all your ducks in a row, and that the only thing
you need to nail the project is money.

I will not provide a full example, because it is pretty easy to imagine
what this section should look like, and also because, when read out of
context, this kind of narrative tends to be boring. Generally, for each chapter you envision, your proposal should include something like this:

Chapter Three argues that _____. In
light of work I have already done in my home library, in the
_____ Archives, the _____
Papers, and the Library of _____, there is compelling
reason to believe that _____ did not
really _____, as is widely believed, but rather
actually _____, _____, and,
oddly enough, _____! A further three months
of reading in the Special Collections of the National Library of
_____, and continued exchange with the lively
group of scholars based there, will help me clinch my argument.

A word to the wise: do not copy what I just wrote. Use your own words.

WRAP IT UP, ADD A BOW

In the conclusion, show once again that you know the secondary literature
inside out, and that your book/article/dissertation is going to make a
distinctive contribution to it. Here too the lack of context will make an
example superfluous. Step back, recapitulate your argument, and show
how it will contribute to an already rich body of literature.

In the final paragraph, return ever-so-briefly to your opening narrative,
showing once again how it illuminates big questions. This return-to-the-
beginning-at-the-end trick is called "ring structure." It has been used at
least since Herodotus, and remains in widespread use today for one very
simple reason: it is extremely effective. It gives a powerful impression of
completeness and resolution. For an example, see the end of this chapter,
where I make a nifty allusion to the Thanksgiving dinner I began with.

For another example, consider the heartrending first and last paragraphs of a study of school desegregation in Boston by J. Anthony Lukas
called *Common Ground: A Turbulent Decade in the Lives of Three American Families*, which
won the Pulitzer Prize, National Book Award, and National Book Critic's
Circle award:

Sunlight struck the gnarled limbs outside his window, casting a
thicket of light and shadow on the white clapboards. From his desk
high under the eaves, Colin Diver could watch students strolling the
paths of Cambridge Common or playing softball on the neatly

trimmed diamond. It was one of those brisk afternoons in early spring, the kind of day which in years past had lured him into the dappled light, rejoicing in his good fortune. But here he lurked in his study walled in by books, overcome by doubt.[12]

And then the devastating final paragraph, 648 pages later, describing the suburban house that Diver has recently bought:

> The most distinctively Colonial feature of the house was a white picket fence which flanked it on both sides. Constructed at the turn of the century, the fence was built in the seventeenth century style without a single nail, its balusters and rails fitted together with mortise and tenon, a square peg in a square hole; but with years of neglect, it had sagged and buckled for yards at a stretch. Colin set out to rebuild it. All that winter in his basement workshop he cut hundreds of new balusters, 1 3/8 inches square, topped by an ornamental molding. Then he ripped dozens of new rails, three inches high and nine feet long. With saw and file he cut the mortises, keeping them 1/32 of an inch smaller than the tenons to guarantee a snug joint. When spring came, he spent evenings and weekends fitting the pieces together, then laying on three coats of white paint. In early June the job was done, the intricate junction of peg and hole sealing off the Divers' perimeter, rearing its ivory spine against the world.[13]

On the first page, Diver is hopeful, energized, and yet doubtful, looking out the window and onto society, the intermingled light and shadow suggesting that whites and blacks might be able to intermingle in Boston's complicated neighborhoods. By the end of the book, after a decade of brutal politics, racial violence, and failed attempts to break down the walls of prejudice, things have changed. Diver has retreated to the suburbs, taking his family far from their old home in the middle of town. Rather than looking out onto society and hoping to change it for the better, Diver is looking inward and thinking only about his house. In the beginning, sunlight and shadow, hope and doubt, black and white, were mixed. Now the white picket fence, rearing its unshadowed ivory spine against the world, forms a defensive barrier around Diver and his family. Hope has been defeated along with the promise of desegregation. Lukas's artful metaphors playing on black and white, light and shadow, nail home in the reader's mind that the story they've just read is a tragedy.

A FEW GENERAL THOUGHTS ON STYLE

- Your proposal should be correct in every way. Its grammar, syntax, spelling, and format should be flawless. If possible, use letterhead. Make your application sparkle.
- Be efficient. Do not attempt to impress readers with your sesquipedalian vocabulary. They are not interested. They are slogging through huge piles of proposals. They want maximum brilliance expressed in the minimum number of syllables. I could give you an example of efficient writing beyond what I've already tried to do throughout this book, but it wouldn't be efficient to do so, so I won't.
- You should favor vivid, concrete, sensually evocative language. You might think that your readers will respect abstract language because it will bespeak the importance of your project. But you would be wrong. Your readers are human beings. They enjoy good writing. So, for example, you could write:

In multiple surveys, interpreted, of course, from a subjective-hermeneutical rather than an objective-empirical standpoint, large numbers of Highly Educated Grant-Making Professionals (HEGMPs, hereafter) have reported not only acutely soporific ramifications stemming from their core-competency-related analytical activities, but, indeed, not-infrequent episodes of involuntary peristaltic eruption (See Figure 4.3b). One HEGMP went so far as to conjecture the imminent emergence of a novel specialization in the field of behavioral economics: i.e., "Suboptimal Academic Language Deployment Behaviors Under Conditions of Paramount Career-Path-Transformative Competition."

Or you could write this:

Much of the academic writing that grant officers read makes them want to puke. "What the fuck is wrong with you people?" one recently yelled at a half-finished pile of fellowship applications. "There is serious money on the table here! I'll tell you what I'll give you a goddamned *grant* for: explain to me why academics write such unreadable *crap!*"

You decide which approach is more effective. (For the record, you should probably leave swear words out of your grant application.) Here's an example of the kind of evocative writing I am talking about. It is from Voyaging, the first volume of Janet Browne's magisterial biography of Charles Darwin. On a hike through the Andes,

There was a transparency in the air and a stillness that gave [Darwin] the sensation of being in another world. . . . The illusion continued as his travelling party climbed up over the passes through the perpetual snow. Intense colour was the most unexpected thing, said Darwin. On each side there stood bold conical hills of red granite, intersected by the deep blue of a glacier—not thought to occur in these mountains. Vast piles of purple detritus spilled into the valleys making their own mountains thousands of feet high. The moon and stars were magical, the clouds silver, the rising sun a giant orange disc divided by a distant horizon as level as the ocean; and the profundity of the sky was everything Humboldt had ever described. As the party sat round the evening campfire, Darwin's flannel waistcoat added to the fantastical effect by crackling with static electricity in the dark. Even the baggage mules left coloured footsteps behind them: not blood as Darwin first thought, nor dust from the red porphyritic rocks, but from countless airborne spores of a lichen crushed underfoot. On their return across the Uspallata pass, there were "white, red, purple & green sedimentary rocks & black lavas . . . broken up by hills of porphyry of every shade of brown & bright lilacs. All together they were the first mountains which I had seen which literally resembled a coloured geological section."[14]

Browne does not simply tell you that Darwin's journey was extraordinary. She shows you, by evoking the colors, the textures, the amazing sights Darwin saw, and the thoughts they inspired in Darwin's magnificent mind. In this gorgeous passage, we can see how Charles Lyell's theories of geological change were made real for Darwin on this epic walk through the mountains. Concrete detail is connected in every phrase to the larger issues that Darwin, and Browne are thinking through. Browne demonstrates that is possible to write about complex ideas in lush, evocative language. That should be your goal too.

- On style guides: there are many mediocre to downright bad guides to writing on the market. This is because even a moderately successful short guide to writing can make a small fortune for its author. Which is exactly why—well, never mind. But if there is one book you consult on matters of style, I recommend *A Writer's Companion* by Richard Marius. It is witty, opinionated, beautifully evocative, and above all, a pleasure to read. I like the sharp-edged third edition more than the somewhat sanded-down fourth. But both are excellent.[15]

WORKSHOP

Let us return to the Thanksgiving dinner at the beginning of this chapter. Whereas in that instance you were cooking for your grant-proposal-evaluating guests, in this one, your writing group will take their place, providing insights about your braised carrots and other delicious holiday fare . . . or rather, about your exquisitely crafted proposal.

Here is how I suggest it should go. Once you have completed your draft, distribute it in electronic form to the other members of your writing group about a week before your meeting. If there are between two and five of you, everyone can read everyone else's proposal. If there are more, you should break into smaller groups such that each member reads a manageable number of proposals. One way of tying the whole group together is for each person to read the proposals of the three people whose names follow theirs in alphabetical order. Allan's proposal will thus be read by Barry, Cathy, and Deborah. Yancey's proposal will be read by Zelda, Allan, and Barry, and so on.

However you organize the workshop, everyone should meet at once, so that all can benefit from hearing the critiques and praise you give one another. It is important that everyone receive both criticism and praise. As you go around the table, discussing each proposal in turn, each participant should receive both positive and negative comments. I recommend that, for every proposal you read, you offer three specific items of praise and three equally specific items of critique. That way each participant will both be encouraged and given concrete ways of improving their work.

After the meeting is over, give yourselves a break. Then take a few additional weeks to revise, tweak, and finally polish your proposals before sending them to your external evaluators, about whom you will learn next, in Chapter 13.

Chapter 13

SOLICIT HONEST, HELPFUL FEEDBACK

When I last ran the grant-writing workshop that became this book, about eighteen people were at the first meeting, but only eight persisted to the end. Once all eight had finished a polished draft of their grant proposals, we sent those drafts to three people: David Wrobel and David Chappell, who hold endowed chairs in the University of Oklahoma History Department, and are experts in Western American history and African American history, and Marcia Folsom, who was in town by a coincidence, and is an expert on English literature, with extensive publications on Jane Austen and other topics. Among her other distinctions, Folsom also happens to be my mom.

Pretending to be an eccentric billionaire who was funding the grant competition and making the rules, I asked the committee to read all the proposals and select the top three for funding. The top grant would supposedly get fifty thousand dollars, second place would receive twenty-five-thousand, and the third-place winner would walk away with ten thousand pretend smackaroos.

We all then sat down around a table on my back porch. I asked the grant-making committee to discuss all the proposals as they would in a real selection committee, imagining that the authors were absent. It was nerve-racking for the participants, especially before the discussion began. But as the conversation about the merits and flaws of each proposal moved forward, it became clear to all the participants that the committee members were being fair and respectful of each candidate, and that they felt very impressed by the work that went into all the proposals. This was so for several reasons. One is that all three of the committee members are smart, caring, wonderful people. Another is that they have been on the other side of the evaluation process a thousand times, and they knew how hard, how important, and how stressful it is. Nobody said vicious things about any proposal. All had good things to say about every proposal. Choices about whom to give the pretend money turned on who was furthest along in their work, who seemed best prepared, and whose project was most focused. The worst thing said about any of the proposals was that it was not ready yet.

In the end, despite many differences in taste and opinion, the committee was unanimous in its selection of the top proposal. It was Bryan Rindfleisch's " 'Possessed of the Most Extensive Trade, Connexions, and Influence': The Atlantic Intimacies of an Eighteenth-Century Indian Trader," which deals with native peoples in the old South and their engagement with the Atlantic mercantile economy. It was the proposal for which the most research had been completed, and it addressed the most ambitious set of historical questions. The committee also agreed on the runner up, Rowan Steineker, whom we've met before, then petitioned the billionaire funder of this competition to ask if they could split the remaining ten thousand dollars into two five-thousand-dollar dissertation-development grants. He agreed. The writers asked the committee a variety of questions, before we adjourned our meeting to relax over beer and wine.

Despite the stress of having their work evaluated in the open, the group had established a great deal of trust over the course of the workshop, and knew that they would not be judged cruelly, either by the committee or their peers. Moreover, the participants agreed that the meeting had been useful, for a variety of reasons. For those whose work was selected for pretend money, it was a shot in the arm. And for those whose work was not selected, the discussion among the committee members had been even more valuable: it helped them see a clear path to improving their work, since they knew precisely why their proposal was not selected and others were. Since that meeting, every one of the participants, both those who won the fake money and those who didn't, has received substantial grants, ranging from a thousand to thirty thousand dollars.

It would certainly be easy to skip this step, and I'm sure you and your group may have other ways of achieving similar or better results. But I urge you to do it nonetheless, because it is enormously useful to get a sense of how deliberations on grant proposals go. If you have a clear and vivid sense of what your readers are looking for, it can guide your writing in useful ways. It is also tremendously valuable to compete and lose when there is only pretend money on the table, so that you can more effectively compete and win when the money is real.

All you need are two or three outside readers, preferably senior faculty members, but junior ones will do. So will graduate students. It is desirable to have people from different fields in the humanities and social sciences represented on the committee, because that is usually how it is in real grant-making committees. The key thing is to have a fresh set of eyes looking at the proposals, and to have people do the hard work of deciding which proposals are strongest. Announcing that there will be refreshments afterward signals that the exchange will be cordial, and that no one should say anything that will wreck the after-party.

Once all this is done, I recommend that you put your proposal aside for a couple of days, then come back to it for some tweaking and polishing as you prepare to share it with the world.

Part IV

INTERVIEWS WITH EXPERTS

Chapter 14

JAMES F. BROOKS

A professor of history and anthropology at the University of California, Santa Barbara, James F. Brooks is an interdisciplinary scholar of the indigenous and colonial past, and has held professorial appointments at the University of Maryland and University of California, Berkeley, as well as fellowships at the Institute for Advanced Study in Princeton and the School for Advanced Research (SAR) in Santa Fe. In 2002 he became director of SAR Press, and between 2005 and 2013 served as president of SAR. He recently completed three years as chair of the board of directors of the Western National Parks Association, which supports research, preservation, and education in sixty-seven national parks, including Bandelier National Monument, Chaco Culture National Historical Park, and Channel Islands National Park. He is also a trustee of the Santa Bárbara Mission Archive-Library, as well as the Santa Barbara Trust for Historic Preservation.

Brooks is the recipient of numerous national awards for scholarly excellence. His 2002 book *Captives and Cousins: Slavery, Kinship and Community in the Southwest Borderlands* focused on the trafficking of women and children across New Mexico as expressions of intercultural violence and accommodation. He has also published the edited volumes

Confounding the Color Line: The Indian-Black Experience in North America (2002),
Women and Gender in the American West (2004), Small Worlds: Method, Meaning,
and Narrative in Microhistory (2008), and Keystone Nations: Indigenous Peoples and
Salmon in the North Pacific (2012). His 2016 book, Mesa of Sorrows: A History of
the Awat'ovi Massacre, seeks to understand an eruption of violence that
occurred among the Hopis in the year 1700.[1]

What role have grants and fellowships played in your career?

They are transformative. The great institutes, like the Institute for Advanced
Study in Princeton, the Omohundro Institute for Early American History
and Culture, and the School of Advanced Research in Santa Fe, both release
you from teaching and provide you with communities of scholars with
whom you can reflect and share knowledge and ideas.

The first grant I got was a five-hundred-dollar undergraduate research
grant from the University of Colorado that allowed me to go to Trinidad,
Colorado, and Purgatory River Valley to do research on Hispano coal min-
ers, research that many years later became Captives and Cousins. I found that
some of these families had Indian captives in their families, and that was
what launched my project. So grants provide peace of mind, time to do
research, and a community of scholars.

At the SAR, we had on average 120 applications a year for six positions.
Our process was just as rigorous as Harvard's, since we had a 5 percent
take rate. The single biggest mistake our applicants made was to write as if
the application was going to be read by people only within their particular
area of specialization. That is not how review committees are composed.
We always had all four fields of anthropology represented on our committees: archaeology, linguistics, sociocultural, and biological. Then we would
have one outside person, a historian or sociologist or political scientist. If
you wrote your proposal as if it were for people in your own subfield, it
would bore the hell out of nonspecialists. Like, why bother me with some
seventeenth-century map you're studying when I am trying to understand
the origins of humankind?

I coach people to open their application with "why your project matters." Whether you are in humanities, public humanities, or social sciences, you have to show why any taxpayer or philanthropist would care
about the project. Applicants should imagine the readers of the grant proposal as a full history department, for instance. You'll have someone who

does early modern Europe, a student of late antiquity, someone who does twentieth-century United States, and someone who does medieval China reading your proposal. You have to convince them that your project matters to them, too, in that it seeks to answer enduring historical questions.

Are there any examples of a proposal that was very effective in that way?

Well, you begin with a hook that addresses some big human question. One reason I got my first job at Maryland right out of the gate, with the dissertation still unfinished, was because my chair, Dan Calhoun, required me to come up with a single sentence that described why my dissertation was interesting. What I said was, "This is a story of American slavery in a region, and among peoples, we've never thought of as masters of slaves and victims of slavery." When I offered that, the search committee members said, "Oh really? Tell us more!" You should form that sentence as early on in the process of conceiving your dissertation or research project as possible.

In our correspondence you have commented on how things have changed in the grant-making world. Could you elaborate on that?

These changes are particularly salient at the institutional level, if you are applying to the Rockefeller or Ford or NEH [National Endowment for the Humanities] or the Guggenheim foundations, but they are also there at the individual level. Every grant writer ought to keep assessment in mind. By that, I mean, how will you tell if a project is successful? That and accountability. How will the funder know what the "social return on investment" was? If I produce a standard academic monograph, the average number of copies it will sell is five hundred. Lifetime. You have to be able to explain why producing that book is important.

What caused this change? General changes in academia as a whole?

I can tell you very specifically why it changed: Sarbanes-Oxley (2002) and the financial crisis of 2008–2010 (which reverberates still). The law was aimed at corporations and making their boards responsible for their activities. But it trickled out into the nonprofit world. When I served as president of SAR, I noticed our trustees getting increasingly nervous about producing social value. If we are spending public (or private) money, we want to know we are doing something good. Otherwise, we are not doing our job. We don't want to be seen as pissing away a charitable donation. The trustees were now liable for it and held accountable. Trustees became much more concerned about proving we were making a difference.

Is this a good thing? A bad thing? Neutral?

It's the new normal. We live with this now. You have to show that your project will matter. You need to be convinced, and to be convincing, that there are serious constituencies concerned with your topic. Not an academic parlor group or society of dilettanti. For better or for worse, this is the future of scholarship.

It sounds very different from the world of postmodern skepticism about the fabric of reality that I ran into as a student in the 1990s.

The postmodern turn in the 1990s undercut public trust in the academy. People found it impossible to know what academics were talking about, and it alienated academics from the broader public. These days you have to produce work that concerns people and their lived reality. I now serve as editor of *The Public Historian* and spend much of my time thinking, "How can this reach people in the nonacademic world?" "How can we get to the streets, through the public libraries, book clubs, and other forums where we can demonstrate the relevance of what we are doing for real people?" I recently published a trade book that attempts to understand how a massacre occurred in a Hopi village in the fall of 1700. It concerns how communities address violence and trauma, what kinds of things drive this kind of violence, what are people seeking through violence. How can perfectly decent people do perfectly awful things? What are the possibilities for reconciliation?

How is the process of writing a trade book different from writing an academic one?

My editor, John Glusman at W.W. Norton, gave me a simple and very useful line while tutoring me: the job of the trade author is to "make the reader feel smart, not to make the author look smart." In academic writing it's often about being as confusing and obscure as possible, throwing in as much jargon as possible so we can sound "nuanced." What the world wants is a good story, and for the author to be largely invisible.

Is that what grant proposal evaluators want too?

Yes. You want them to be able to say, "Wow! That sounds interesting!" There's a riff I have when talking with graduate students about the "tyranny of historiography." Historiography only matters to historians. Only. I urge people to go into the archives or into the field, read in the historical moment, and find your way into the story. After crafting your sense of the story, only then should they consult the literature. The most important thing is to have a grasp of the narrative arc: the beginning, the middle, and especially the end. It is the opposite of what most graduate programs teach. Karen Halttunen once coached a group of graduate students at UC Davis, "What the world *doesn't* need more of is the much-discussed 'gap in the literature.'" Our typical pedagogy is ancestor worship. It teaches students that their public audience comes second.

A lot of people in the academy are distressed or pessimistic about the kinds of changes you are talking about—the casualization of academic labor, the power and importance of market forces in intellectual life—but you sound somewhat more optimistic. Is that fair?

I think so. If we are bold and open enough to represent ourselves and to talk to fascinating people living complicated lives outside the academy, we can turn it around. What we need is more publicly attentive scholarship. If we try to circle the wagons and protect the way things have always been, we're sunk. The Vikings are already at the door, and they have battle axes. The only way to stop the anti-humanists of the world is to convince taxpaying citizens to want to support what we do, to engage with local archives, museums, and public libraries. For example, the University of Iowa invested in the creation of a mobile museum. They obtained a Winnebago. In that they created a mobile museum and they park it in Wal-Mart parking lots. Some days they have four hundred, five hundred people moving through the exhibits. They bring research faculty and graduate students. It's wonderful. It's an amazing way of engaging the public with academic research.[2]

It seems like a difficult balance for younger scholars to achieve: on the one hand they've got to speak to the world at large, and on the other they've got to speak to colleagues in their specialty.

It is difficult. The political economy of academic promotion is so circuitous and internal. To get tenure, you have to convince the six to ten people who are going to be your external letter writers that you are a fine scholar with "trajectory." There is a great deal of genuflecting to other people's work, lest you alienate your reviewer. We ought not be talking to such a small circle of people; rather, our audience ought to be the interested public who support public universities. It's nobody's fault. It is just the way things have evolved.

So grad students and younger scholars have to both tell a good story and genuflect to authorities if they want to get funded?

Not everyone is able to do it. Prospective students ought to know that as they enter graduate school. They need to know that things have changed. It is no longer an elite social club. We are answerable to a whole new world of constituents. Unless you have a wealthy patron, you have to learn to work in this new landscape. When you are writing, think about the local librarian who helped you do your research when you were a kid. That's the person you want to persuade. If you are able capture her or his attention, you are doing your job.

In working on this book, and listening to you, it has seemed to me that barriers between disciplines matter less and less. Is that a fair assessment?

Well, it holds true for my experience at the SAR in that we were always looking for proposals that spanned disciplines, arced across them. That was very important to the mission to "deepen our understanding of human culture, history, evolution, and creative expression." One of my duties at UC Santa Barbara is to bridge history and anthropology through our public history program. So I would say distinctions between disciplines are less important than are the convergences. Some folks are better able than others to do this. Not many applicants do it well, but some are able. Some have a great talent for it. Take Tiya Miles. She was a postdoc at Berkeley when we published her first piece, "Bone of My Bone," in the *American Indian Quarterly* in 1998. Here's someone who has all the chops as a researcher in archives. But she also has an ear for what matters to the public. Read *The House on Diamond Hill*. It is the model for the future of our scholarship. It earned her a MacArthur Fellowship. She put herself in the story. Parts of it are heart-wrenching. She did an amazing thing. The Vann house is a very historic site. It was on the Cherokee national trail. Everyone worshipped

Chief Vann. Nobody talked about him as a woman abuser, and an owner of slaves. Miles uncovered it and meticulously documented it. Over the course of a decade, she worked with the docents at the House. She did so patiently and gently. She is amazing in conversation with people. In a decade, she completely changed the interpretive narrative of Chief Vann as it is now told at the historic site. It is absolutely brilliant.[3]

One thing that many graduate students struggle with is theory. How do you help your mentees with it?

It depends on what you do. Theory exists to put your work in conversation with others. It is not historiography. It is not a matter of some pissing contest or ancestor worship. Look at Miles's story of a Cherokee slaveholder. What were the similarities and differences between Indian and white slaveholders? Asking that question puts this single case into a much larger conversation.

The best book on this is one I ask all my graduate students to read, by Charles Ragin and Howard Becker, from 1992. It's called *What Is a Case?* It is the most elegant conceptualization of what theory does. You say, "I have a case. It is a case of a slaveholding Cherokee. It deserves my attention and explication. But, then what is it a case of?" Once you ask that question it becomes far larger. It might become global. Is it a case of domestic violence across racial lines? Is it a case of slaveholder privilege? Nonwhite slaveholder privilege? It is a case of God knows how many things. Ragin and Becker are excellent in the way they help you frame your research theoretically.[4]

How do you help graduate students cope with the high rate of failure on the grant and fellowship market?

We've done fairly well at UCSB. We have something around an 85 percent placement rate for our graduate students in academic jobs, but only about half of those are tenure-track. The whole of academia is becoming a segmented labor market. One reason for some of our most successful cases derives from grad seminars that are collaborative and multidisciplinary. We just wrapped one year of such a program: http://www.news.ucsb.edu/2016/016969/bridge-discovery. These are as wide-ranging and conceptually oriented as possible, which makes it possible to cast their work toward speaking with nonspecialists. It's an alternative to a situation like an academic conference where you've got eight people on stage and eight people in the audience, counting the janitor standing in the back. You have to be able to talk about your work in widely compelling ways.

A theme that has come up in numerous conversations I've had has been writing, and the importance of writing for fellowship applications. Can you talk about how you think of writing?

When I was writing *Mesa of Sorrows*, I read nothing but poetry (aside, of course, from the literature that underlay it). It is all about the search for precision and condensed language and emotion and power and beauty. As I was writing, I used a poem every day as my writing prompt.[5]

I don't imagine people often think of "emotion and power and beauty" in the context of grant applications.

It will make a difference if you read fine writing, every day. It will make a difference if you employ it. The late Keith Basso used to say that "we may not be able to teach academics to write beautifully, but we can show them what it looks like." This is one of the reasons we launched the Lannan Literary Arts Program at the SAR. We were dismayed by the lack of "reach" in the academic writing. It was so internal. We received funding from Lannan to bring poets and creative writers in residence to remind people that written and spoken words matter. Not to teach, but to remind.

Chapter 15

LIZABETH COHEN

Lizabeth Cohen is dean of the Radcliffe Institute and Howard
Mumford Jones Professor of American Studies, Department of History,
Harvard University. She is also the author of the 1990 book *Making a
New Deal: Industrial Workers in Chicago, 1919–1939*, which won the Bancroft
Prize in American History and the Philip Taft Labor History Book
Award and was a finalist for the Pulitzer Prize. Her next book, *A
Consumers' Republic: The Politics of Mass Consumption in Postwar America* (2003),
explored how an economy of mass consumption shaped social life,
culture, and politics following World War II. Cohen has published
widely in top history and urban studies journals, winning numerous
awards and distinctions. Her writings have also appeared in edited
collections and popular venues including the *New York Times, Washington
Post*, and *American Prospect*. She is also coauthor with David Kennedy
of a widely used U.S. history college textbook, *The American Pageant*
(2007).[1]

Cohen's current book project, *Saving America's Cities: Ed Logue and the
Struggle to Renew Urban America in the Suburban Age* (forthcoming) considers
the benefits and costs of rebuilding American cities through the life
and career of urban planner Edward J. Logue, who contributed to

major redevelopment projects across the Northeast, including the "New Boston" that emerged in the 1960s.

What advice would you give to applicants to the Radcliffe Institute?

Have you read the book *Thinking Like Your Editor: How to Write Great Serious Nonfiction and Get It Published*? It's a useful book by Susan Rabiner and Alfred Fortunato. It was written by a literary agent and helps writers get into the mind of a publisher. It helps writers know what publishers are looking for. It shows you how to get beyond the disciplinary tropes and categories that people work within, and to connect with broader audiences. It helps you see your own project with new eyes.[2] The review process for fellowships is not very different.

I understand that failure to do just that, to see the project as an outsider, is one of the main mistakes that applicants make.

Yes, particularly young people. They are often so concerned with being credible in their own discipline that they tend to invoke too much jargon and categories of analysis that don't mean much to people outside their fields. The trick is to be credible both within your field and outside of it. Here at the Radcliffe Institute the first reader of an application will be someone who is fairly close to the applicant field-wise. If the applicant gets to be a finalist, the application will then go to a committee [of people who are] more removed from the field. You have to speak to both audiences. Often people do better in the first round, since they work with assumptions that the reviewer is familiar with—whereas at the next level, it's sometimes as if the proposal is written in Greek. Or, the concern at the finalist stage may be that the person is not cutting to the heart of the problem, or may be too trapped in categories of analysis dominant in their field.

When I read a proposal, I want to know immediately that the person is analytical. I don't want her to hide behind a vocabulary that is meaningful only in a small subfield. I want to see that she is really able to explain what the problem is, to probe where the topic fits with other scholarship. You don't need to trash the existing scholarship, or justify your own work by denigrating other people's. You want to show you know how your work will build on that of other scholars; how it matters. That is very important. I want applicants to convince me this is really significant, and to do so in language that is not too limited to where their discipline is right now.

How should applicants balance being ambitious with the practicalities of writing a book?

Some people propose projects that could easily become a ten-volume work. Those projects are not doable. Or they propose something that is so small that it is impossible to see its larger importance. You have to find a sweet spot, where the ambition is clear, but where it is also convincing that you are capable of completing it. Every proposal has to negotiate between showing how ambitious and significant the project is and describing the nitty-gritty, page-by-page experience of the work they hope to write. The key thing is to start the proposal by laying out a big analytical problem you are going to address, and then to dig down into a piece of the project to show how your research speaks to that larger question.

I was interested to hear that the first thing you look for is the analytical quality of the proposal. I've been surprised to hear the opposite from a number of people. Several people I've spoken with have emphasized the importance of the quality of the writing and of showing the project's human interest.

It is not either-or. People are right in that the writing tells you something about how effective the student or professor will be. To a certain extent, what you see is what you get. If the proposal is badly written, you don't have a lot of confidence in the candidate. By badly written, I also mean sloppy. A proposal that doesn't present well doesn't inspire confidence. If you have a word limit and the proposal comes in twice as long, that's a problem.

As for human interest, as historians we look for the telling anecdote, or the hook. That is fine. I am not a narrative historian, but I've seen that done effectively many times. But I also watch review committees across fields. In the humanities and social sciences, I don't think people are looking for narrative and human drama so much as they are looking for the significance and the analytical contribution the work will make. That is what is most important. Reviewers are not just looking for a good story. They are looking for what makes the story important. It is fine for applicants to tell a story, but I want to be confident that the applicant knows why the story matters, and how it will change the way we think about an important analytical problem.

Theory often trips up younger scholars. How should they handle it?

That is hard to answer, since it varies with different fields. In certain social sciences, for example, the contribution needs to be theoretical. But that is not always so. Evaluators need to know that the applicant is aware of theory and sees beyond the specifics of the case. When I say "analytical," theory is part of that. There are many ways of showing analytical or theoretical sophistication. However you do it, you need to show how your work is informed by some theoretical readings. Theory helps frame the problem and helps applicants show how their research has implications beyond their subfield.

I have been struck by how consensus-driven much of the decision-making is in selection committees. Is that your impression as well?

There are certainly differences of opinion, but people on our selection committees generally get along. There is a certain amount of horse trading that goes on. The surprise for me is more at how loudly quality speaks. It matters less what the discipline is. People generally recognize important work. People at the top of their field usually are able to see quality across disciplines.

How do you help students and junior colleagues cope with the competitiveness of the grant and fellowship application process?

I tell them to apply for a lot of things, and don't expect any one of them to come through. One of the ironies or contradictions that does run through this process is that often the strongest proposals come from people who are near the end of their projects. That works against junior people. People who are farther along in their project know what they are doing. They know what problem they are solving, or what question they are answering. It is harder for someone at the beginning of a project to articulate it in the terms that application reviewers are looking for. That first struck me years ago when I was on an NEH panel for the first time. I knew a lot of the people whose work we were reviewing. And I knew their books were practically done. Ironically, we were giving people money to finish one book and to start a new one. You are in a stronger position if you are farther along with your project.

So what do you tell young people who are just starting their research?

One thing I would say is to be aware of where you are applying. At the Radcliffe Institute we are building a class of fifty fellows who are diverse in terms of rank. We have a track record of taking some people who are untenured, but we don't always do so. Applicants should not waste their time applying for grants that are not intended for them. You should look for fellowships at places where there are people like you. Another thing I would mention that comes up with my own students is that, as soon as you can, it is to your benefit to transition from having your dissertation advisers and committee members write for you to having people in your field write for you. Your advisers are like your parents, and for that reason they are not as trustworthy. If the only letters you have are coming from the people who raised you in the field, it is not as credible as when you get two letters from people who reviewed your manuscript or commented on your article, or were commentators on a panel you were on and were really impressed. That gets the message across really powerfully, much more so than do letters from your dissertation advisers. The other thing about advisers is that, over time, they are less and less in touch with your work. The letter starts to look dated, as it is built around your earlier work. If you get letters from people you meet as you are making your mark in the profession, that speaks powerfully about what you have achieved.

On the topic of recommendations, I think there is widespread ignorance among graduate students and younger scholars about recommenders: whom to ask, and how to treat them. What would you tell them about what I call "recommender management"?

That is a good question. Sometimes I have former students who ask me to write for them and they don't send me their proposal. I need to know what I am recommending. The letter needs to be specific. I will ask them for the proposal, and they say, "I'm still working in it." Then they send it to me a day before the recommendation is due. There is no time to tailor the letter. Applicants have to plan very strategically. They have to get the proposal done in time for recommenders to read it and think about it. I hate getting a request for a letter a week before it is due. There isn't time to do it well. I hate to say no, but I will be very resentful about their not being respectful of my time. The materials for the application should not dribble in to the recommender bit by bit. Everything—the CV, the pro-posal, the writing sample, the addressed envelopes—should all arrive at once. Right now, I am marching through a list of letters that I am writing. I set up time on the side to work on each batch. I don't want to go back to add material once I've got the letter written.

Have the research priorities of the Radcliffe Institute changed over time?

Maybe they have in particular years. But aside from that, excellence re-mains the standard across years. That is defined differently across fields. There are some things like the internationalization of history that become fashionable, and reviewers are likely to recognize that. There are other is-sues that vary from year to year. For instance, say there are two applicants in related fields and one is very senior and has done important work for many years, and has published great books. They are applying for a late-career book that is more synthetic and less rooted in archival work. We are a residential fellowship and there are real benefits to having such a person here to mentor junior scholars. If you compare a senior scholar to a younger applicant who does not have as much of a track record but has a lot of promise, it is a hard choice. There is a lot of disagreement on which person to accept. Some will want to bring the senior person and invest in enriching the community. Others will want to bring the younger scholar because they think we should be supporting younger people. Those are disagreements that get resolved in different ways from year to year.

I've been struck to hear how many historians are selected in fellowship competitions, and, by comparison, how few literary scholars are. I have heard that literary scholars tend to be more critical of one another's work than scholars in other fields. Is that the case at the Radcliffe Institute?

One of the things we have done to counteract that risk is to control for the differences in how people evaluate. We compare the grade a reviewer as-signs a particular applicant to the average grade that reviewer gives, so that a high score from a hard grader carries more weight than a high score from a reviewer who tends to give many high scores. This is a system we have adapted from the ACLS. As far as history is concerned, the reason we have more historians here than people in any other discipline is that more historians apply than do [scholars] from any other field. I think that's because historians write books and need big hunks of time to finish them.

What distinguishes the Radcliffe Institute from other, similar institutions?

We are the broadest Institute for Advanced Study. We have fellows from the arts, social sciences, hard sciences: writers, painters, composers, literary scholars, nonacademic public intellectuals, journalists. The second point is that we are diverse in rank. The community has people from many career stages. It is helpful for them all. Younger scholars can get mentorship from older ones, and senior scholars can get help keeping up with what is going on in their fields. Beyond that, we try to create a community that is both domestic and international, and demographically diverse. We have generally had 60 percent women and 40 percent men. We are not engineering that. We get more applications from women, perhaps because of the reputation of Radcliffe College. People's assumption is that we focus on gender and women, even though that is not what we do. The promotion of research in that area is one of our missions, but it is only one. We have never had more men than women.

One of the scary aspects of our fellowship competition is that we are inundated with applications. Every year the pool grows. We have a 3 to 4 percent acceptance rate. Harvard College accepts 6 percent, so our fellowships are harder to get than admission to Harvard College. It is a sign of how desperate people are to get time away from teaching and administrative duties to return to their research and how appealing it is to participate in a stimulating, multidisciplinary community.

Chapter 16

THOMAS B. F. CUMMINS

A Dumbarton Oaks Professor of Pre-Columbian and Colonial Art at Harvard University, Thomas B. F. Cummins earned his Ph.D. from UCLA in 1988. He taught for eleven years at the University of Chicago and was the director of its Center for Latin American Studies from 1998 to 2001. From 2003 to 2004, he served as acting director of the David Rockefeller Center for Latin American Studies at Harvard. He has lived and taught in Argentina, Colombia, Ecuador and Peru.

Cummins's research and teaching focuses on pre-Columbian and Latin American colonial art. Recent research interests include the 1996 analysis of early Ecuadorian ceramic figurines (*Huellas del Pasado: Los Sellos de Jama-Coaque Banco Central del Ecuador*) and the study of late-pre-Columbian systems of knowledge and representation, especially those of the Inca, and their influence on the formation of sixteenth- and seventeenth-century colonial artistic and social forms (*Toasts with the Inca: Andean Abstraction and Colonial Images on Kero Vessels*, 2002, and *Native Traditions in the Colonial World*, 1992). He has also published essays on New World town planning, early images of the Inca, miraculous images in Colombia, and the relationship between visual and alphabetic literacy in the conversion of Indians. Most recently, he collaborated with a team of scholars at the Getty Research Institute to study two illustrated manuscripts from seventeenth-century Peru. The first volume to result from this work, *The Getty Murúa: Essays on the Making of Martín de Murúa's "Historia General del Piru,"* was co-edited with Barbara Anderson and published by Getty in 2008.[1]

What role have grants played in your career as a researcher?

I've been very fortunate. When I was at UCLA for my doctoral work, there was internal money to help graduate students with their preliminary research. This kind of funding helps people prepare for larger grants later on. Often in larger universities there is seed money for people to go out to do exploratory research, because most often, grad students have not really had a chance to go out and do reconnaissance in the area they intend to do research. They haven't been to archives. They haven't identified primary sources for their work. They haven't explored physically the sites they are going to do work on. So early grants, particularly for summer research, are very important to prepare to apply for larger grants, like a Fulbright, SSRC [Social Science Research Council grant], etcetera, when you need to demonstrate your knowledge of the data and resources you will consult, whether they be archival, museum, architectural, and so on. You need to show that you won't be wasting the first six months of the grant figuring out what the hell you're going to do. I had smaller grants from my undergraduate college, Denison, that sent me to Panama to work with the Kuna Indians, for two summers. I didn't know what I was doing, but you learn. You learn by participating in research. Then UCLA got a large donation to help graduate students that allowed me to work in Peru and explore collections and archives there and elsewhere.

After I finished my dissertation and was working at Arizona State, I was fortunate to be offered a two-year MIT postdoctoral fellowship sponsored by the Getty Foundation and directed by Heather Lechtman. That grant literally changed my world. I had just finished my dissertation, in Peru, and that grant helped me start on a new field: Ecuador, and early pre-Columbian ceramics and the technology behind their production.

That was one of the first major external grants I received. Then I was again fortunate to receive a Getty collaborative grant for a year with Joanne Rappaport. We had met in the archives in Ecuador when I was working on the MIT Fellowship, and we found that we were working on similar issues.

We were focused on the use of archives not as a resource for historians, but as an expanded field of literacy, and that took us out into the communities where documents were kept and used for a variety of purposes. We proposed the grant to the Getty five years later as a collaborative project that ended up producing *Beyond the Lettered City*, which won several awards. The Modern Language Association awarded it the Katherine Singer Kovács Prize for an outstanding book published in English or Spanish in the field of Latin American and Spanish literatures and cultures, and it also received the Bryce Wood Book Award, LASA's [Latin American Studies Association's] prize for the outstanding book on Latin America in the social sciences and humanities published in English.

I later had another Getty grant, this time from the Getty Research Institute—I've had a lot of Getty funding, actually. It was a residential grant, which I generally don't like as much since I like to be out in the field. In this case we were working on the Murúa manuscripts with Juan Ossio, where we got to spend a year with a manuscript that no one had ever studied, except for Juan and the owner. We were able to do a collaborative study with people from the research institute, involving myself and Juan and other people we brought in—museum people and conservation people—to do a forensic study. Nothing like it had ever been done before. A Danish librarian had attempted a codicological study using a facsimile Juan Ossio and I had produced, but you can't really do a codicological study on a facsimile or any other kind of technical study. We were fortunate that we had the most sophisticated equipment and colleagues at the Getty so as to produce a fully integrated and innovated study.

Those are the major grants I've gotten. I haven't applied for many, mainly because the institutions where I've worked have supported my research. I've had sabbaticals that have been very productive. I'm about to apply for the Guggenheim. We'll see how that goes.

One theory of mine that your narrative seems to confirm is that in these matters, money attracts money.

I'm not sure I agree with that. It is the production that produces money. If you use grants wisely and expeditiously, and produce something that people respect and are really engaged by, that kind of success will allow you to ride on to the next grant. There are people who get grants and do nothing with them. But that usually doesn't happen.

What do you tell people who haven't had the support they need to produce work that they can then use to help them get grants?

It is more difficult to produce work if you work at a labor-intensive university where you have to do a lot of teaching and advising work. It depends on what kind of career you want. I've never thought of myself as a very driven person. My wife tells me, "Don't kid yourself." If you want to engage at a level in which you can produce work that will allow you to go onto the next project, then you have to burn the midnight oil. You have to sacrifice a lot of things. Time with family. Time for yourself to relax. Because you're always going from one thing to the next. Teaching, advising, writing grants, writing an article, writing your book. There are only so many hours in a week, and most of it gets used that way. There is a great myth that scholars as people with summers and Christmas off have it easy with lots of free time. Everyone I know works their asses off. If we were paid by the hour it would be below minimum wage.

For people who are just getting started with grant proposal writing, what can you tell them about the process of peer review?

Let me tell you about the committees I've sat on. There was one year where it seems like that was all I did. I sat down at the end of it and counted the millions of dollars I had disbursed that year. All I did was read grants. I worked for the Center for Advanced Studies in Visual Art adjudicating applications for scholars to come from Latin America. I've evaluated applications for Dumbarton Oaks forever. Then I was director of the center at Chicago, [where] I was a first reviewer for multiple grants. Fulbrights and SSRCs. Then a reviewer for the Getty Foundation as well. What the hell else was I on? The Millard-Meiss, which is for subventions for books for the College Arts Association, which is important for art historians because it provides money for permissions for photographs for publication. Those are the major things I've done. I also do preliminary review for the Center for Advanced Studies at Princeton, and the Radcliffe Center for Advanced Studies, as well as applications for visiting scholars at the David Rockefeller Center for Latin American Studies (DRCLAS) at Harvard.

Each committee is different. Everyone on the review committee will get the applications. In large pools there is a preliminary review that will whittle them down to x amount of people for the next stage. Fulbright and SSRC do that, as does the ACLS [and] the Societies of Fellows at Harvard,

Princeton, and Columbia. The applications will first go to people in their field who will take a look to see if it really is cutting edge, not in the topic, but in the approach. Is it innovative in the way it is going about it? These latter fellowships are extremely competitive, but also prestigious and lucrative. They are for two to three years. Coming out of graduate school they are really important for people in the humanities and social sciences, especially because most places are making an effort to cut down the time to degree. They allow you to get your book in shape and to start a new project. It is very important to propose a new project for any of these societies of fellows. It's a given that you'll revise your dissertation into a book. But it's critical to have a new project you are getting started on.

It's crucial to do that, and the second project has to be different from what you've just done in your dissertation. If all you propose is to extend your current project into something that's closely related, that will always get shot down and tossed into the reject pile. It very rarely flies to propose something closely related to your current project.

Are there examples of excellent grant proposals that stand out in your mind?

I've read literally thousands of them, between applications to grad school and grant proposals, so it is hard to point to any specific example. I will say this: the first paragraph of any proposal has to be precise. Intellectually driven. Free of any jargon. And with the anticipation that someone who doesn't know the field can at least engage with the intellectual project. Too many proposals are very insular and provincial. And they begin by expanding in a very precise way on the minutia of the project. If you are not already interested in that particular project, that kind of proposal is not very interesting. That is a great problem of some grant writing.

Of course, you have to show you know the field, have command of it. But I am talking about people beginning with the nitty gritty of town planning of a specific Maya site, or something like that. Unless you prove that it has a larger set of issues that it will contribute to then nine of ten grants that are written that way won't get very far. The same is the case if you're working on Pontormo. If you're so jazzed about the archives you've discovered revealing his incestuous relationship with his grandmother, that is great. But nobody cares. It's interesting anecdotally. It's wonderful to have discovered that. But unless you show its relevance to a larger context, it usually won't fly.

So how do applicants do that? By a reference to theory?

It can be by reference to theory. It depends on how you approach the project. You have to be able to sit down and explain what the project is and what its relevance is to the field. The same is true of job interviews. You have to show why scholars outside your field will want to read your work or have you as a member of the department. If you can't, you won't get the job. The proposal also has to have a certain clarity to it. What I tell graduate students is, if you can't explain it to your mother, forget it. That's true for physicists as well. You have to show what you want to achieve and why. She doesn't have to understand physics. But she's got to understand why the project is significant.

What are some of the most common mistakes that grant applicants make?

One issue that is hard to remedy is this: very bad writing.

What does bad writing mean to you?

It means you can't write a good proposal, a clearly defined logical set of sentences that lead one to the next in really pristine prose, in which every word is carefully chosen to mean exactly what you are trying to convey. Any time a word actually doesn't need to be there, it must be taken out. Here, I think, reading someone like Hemingway is a very good lesson. I tell graduate students, you have to read literature. Much academic writing is very bad. I'm serious. For grant writing, Hemingway is an excellent guide. He struggled over every word he wrote. Does it need to be there? Not just the content but the form. I can't tell you how many times I've put down grant proposals and said, I just can't stand reading this. I'm not the only one who says this. I ask myself, am I being prejudiced? But no, nine times out of ten, someone else on the committee will say, "I can't stand reading this either." You'll never get anywhere in academia if you don't write well—actually that's not true. Tons of academic writing is poorly written. But it won't have staying power.

Are there other mistakes that make certain applications easy to eliminate?

A colloquial style doesn't work too well. This is professional activity. You have to treat it that way. Another thing: if the application asks for a bibliography, you'd better know your bibliography. You'd better be up to date. If you know who is on the committee, if you're anywhere close to their field, you need to know what they have written, and what they cite. You don't have to cite it. But you have to know what is there. I've seen it often, where someone on the committee will say the author of this proposal doesn't know this major book in the field. Especially if you are applying to work abroad, and you don't cite the scholarship produced by scholars in that country, that will sink you right off the bat.

In the evaluation of topics centered in foreign countries, that is where writing and precision are most important. If you can't explain it in the abstract to someone outside the field, you will not get too far. What will happen in a committee meeting, if a project sounds good, I will defer to someone else who knows more about the topic than I do. I say, "This makes this topic sound really good. But am I being fleeced here?" Each committee works differently: some will go around the table and give a numerical ranking to each proposal. With others you send in rankings ahead of time and then see how it plays out. With others, you do that, and then that's not the end of it. You discuss the proposals and then rank them again. But in those discussions, I often defer to someone who knows more than I do.

Is the ambitiousness of the proposal important to you?

Yes. But it doesn't have to be big to be ambitious. You can have a small topic that can be incredibly valuable. But to be fundable, it has to have a big impact.

What is the importance of the team of recommenders and peers behind each applicant?

I would say that it is very important, but that it precedes the grant writing. If you do not have a community [of people] with whom you can share ideas, who support your ideas and scholarship prior to grant writing, don't bother applying. When you're a beginning scholar it is so intimidating. I remember being incredibly intimidated. I thought, "Why would anyone want to talk with me?" But there are people who are incredibly generous to younger scholars. Sabine MacCormack was extremely supportive of me. There were others. That's really important. It is hard for beginning students. Some are too aggressive and others are too shy. It's something you have to learn.

What can you say about the competitiveness and the high rate of failure most applicants face?

I used to keep a drawer filled with rejection letters. I'd show them to students. It's a crap shoot. Because someone else got the grant and you didn't—it doesn't mean anything. It's the same for jobs as for grants. Don't begrudge the person their grant. You have to work with these people. Of course you'll like some and not others. It is competitive in the sense that you're all being judged. It's yours to lose by not doing as intellectually rigorous a work as you could. If you can't do it as well as someone else, just accept it and move on. Just try to work up to your capacities. My family has always wanted me to write a book called *Last in His Class*. I failed out of schools. I was a terrible undergrad. I was a terrible grad student, at the beginning. Failures are a great way to learn.

Is there anything we haven't covered that we should have?

One thing is that each fellowship has its parameters. Be very keyed to them. On the other hand—and this is also true of job applications—you have to be true to yourself. Don't try to fake it and say what you think people want to hear. That is always so transparent.

Chapter 17

ANTHONY GRAFTON

The special interests of Anthony Grafton, Henry Putnam University
Professor of History, lie in the cultural history of Renaissance Europe,
the history of books and readers, the history of scholarship and
education in the West from antiquity to the nineteenth century, and
the history of science from antiquity to the Renaissance. He joined the
Princeton History Department in 1975 after earning his A.B. (1971)
and Ph.D. (1975) in history from the University of Chicago and
spending a year at University College London, where he studied with
Arnaldo Momigliano. Grafton likes to see the past through the eyes
of influential and original writers, and has accordingly written
intellectual biographies of a fifteenth-century Italian humanist,
architect, and town planner, Leon Battista Alberti; a sixteenth-century
Italian astrologer and medical man, Gerolamo Cardano; and a
sixteenth-century French classicist and historian, Joseph Scaliger.
He also studies the long-term history of scholarly practices, such as
forgery and the citation of sources, and has worked on many other
topics in cultural and intellectual history. Grafton is the author of ten
books and the coauthor, editor, coeditor, or translator of nine others.
Two collections of essays, *Defenders of the Text* (1991) and *Bring Out Your Dead*

(2001), cover most of the topics and themes that appeal to him. He has received a Guggenheim Fellowship (1989), the *Los Angeles Times* Book Prize (1993), the Balzan Prize for History of Humanities (2002), and the Mellon Foundation's Distinguished Achievement Award (2003), and he is a member of the American Philosophical Society and the British Academy. In 2011 he served as president of the American Historical Association.[1]

Could you talk a little bit about your experience as both an applicant for grants and an evaluator of applications?

I have been applying for grants since the fall of 1970 when I first applied for honorific grants for graduate school. So after forty-five years, I do have some experience with grant applications. I have received support from many agencies and foundations. I have also been on many grant-giving committees, including the governing committee for our own society of fellows at Princeton. I ran the selection for a major research center for two years, and I have been on the committees for two others. I have also been on a selection committee for a major government grant-making agency, the NEH.

Many of the findings of Michèle Lamont's book [*How Professors Think*] were very recognizable. The committees work very hard. They make a real effort to be fair, without being explicit about how it is possible to be fair when you are comparing apples and oranges and pomegranates. This is especially true when committees meet more than once. The committee develops its own language, a sort of shorthand, that makes the evaluation process move more smoothly. In the end, these committees tend to have some feeling of justified confidence that the process is working well, and is not guided by some sort of collective folly.

I have very occasionally watched committee members who see themselves as a sort of disciplinary representative, and push to fund projects in their own discipline. Slightly more often than that I've seen people who were a little bit deaf to other disciplines. That is inevitable to a degree. It's also the reason why committees have various disciplines represented on them.

Lamont's book seemed to me like a pretty optimistic take on the grant evaluation process, particularly in contrast to Bourdieu's darker view.

It would be wrong to put a Foucauldian or Bourdieuvian reading on this, as if people serve on those committees to win power. In reality, you have very little power. You are one of six or eight or twelve people on the committee. And maybe once per round you have the opportunity to make a push that influences how funding is allocated.

If it's not for power, why do people serve on those committees?

It's civic mindedness. They have all had grants, and they have enjoyed amazing years made possible by them, or summers when they were able to remake their dissertation into a book. People know that if this thing of ours, as we say in New Jersey, is to keep on going, we have to do this work. Because if we don't do it, some horrible bureaucratic protocol will be invoked to replace us.

What are the qualities that make a successful grant application?

The first thing you need is a very good elevator speech about your project. You have got to be able to explain to people outside of your area of specialization, in under three minutes, what your project is and why it is interesting and important. The presence or absence of that sharp, effective short description of the project is what most often separates those who get funding from those who do not. Many factors play a role. What school you come from is important. So are the recommendations. So are the samples of work that you supply. But the ability to say what you are doing and why is overwhelmingly important. Many people don't have that mastery. It is often something that develops in the course of writing your dissertation. But often people can't give a really vivid, cogent account of what their project is until well after the dissertation is complete.

What advice do you have on how to manage recommendations?

They are very important. The first and most important thing is to have people writing for you who know you and your work. I am well known and people often come to me and ask me for a recommendation thinking that my name will help them. I try to discourage them, saying, "Look, the problem here is that you took one course with me and you did fine. But you have other people who know you much better. Having my name, and letterhead, and a page and a half of fluff in your file is not going to do much for you. It is much better to have three pages of precise, detailed information from some unknown assistant professor." I tell people that lots of people I recommend do not get the grants they are applying for.

They think that my name will act as some kind of magic talisman. It won't. That is true for graduate admissions, fellowships, and job applications. The crucial thing is to get recommendations from people who know you and can give precise, vivid information about you.

Another thing that is very important to bear in mind is that you should change your recommenders over time. Many of us have our undergraduate mentors and our graduate mentors writing for us for years. On occasion, I will write for some someone who worked with me as an undergraduate, if he or she stays in my field and I am delighted to continue supporting them. But if you do that, you've got to keep your mentor up to date on what you are doing. They can't magically know where you are four years on. When you are a graduate student it is hard to put yourself imaginatively into the role of the mentor. But it is important to try, and to keep in contact with the person over time. If you want an older mentor to write for you, you've got to keep them informed about what you are doing.

When I was out of graduate school and became more senior, I started to rely on contemporaries to write for me. Unfortunately, my older professors all died off, so I couldn't continue to ask them. May all your professors live on to a hundred and twenty and continue to be able to write letters. But you have to ask yourself, is this still the right person to recommend me? We grow old, we retire, many—though not all—of us lose touch with the profession and its ever-changing language.

I've never understood why people don't get new recommenders. Never ask someone for a letter if you are not in regular contact with him or her. You don't have to do it daily. But once or twice a year, send an email, let them know what you are doing, include a pdf of your latest article. From the recommender's point of view, I am a little offended if someone asks me for a letter but doesn't send me a pdf of their latest articles.

This is something people really need to know.

I couldn't agree more. I've told many a very smart person that I couldn't write for them, simply because I did not know enough about their work. I don't tell them I am offended that they asked. I say, "If you can't find someone better to write for you, I'll do it. But there are others who are much better acquainted with what you are doing. Really think about this. You don't want a letter based on a graduate course you took with me in 1988." I try to be gentle and friendly and funny about it. But people asking for letters need to know that they have a duty in this relationship. It is a duty to keep in touch. I'm not talking about having a beer at the AHA [American Historical Association . . .].

Another thing is that the recommender needs to be still active. People are working longer than they used to. I am sixty-five. Within fifteen years I will be eighty. I will have been retired for eight to ten years. I may do some new research and take a new direction just because I have the opportunity to. It's possible I could write a good letter for a former student at age eighty. But I wouldn't bet on it.

I've heard of senior scholars retiring specifically because they didn't want to write any more letters.

I still find writing letters challenging and interesting. Some of my former students recently organized a celebration of my sixty-fifth birthday, and one of them did some background research and counted all the graduate students I've worked with. I have directed forty-six dissertations and have been on about 130 dissertation committees. And I write regularly for the majority of those people.

I've seen some very negative recommendation letters. How does that happen?

It's not something you see often. In a job search with eighty candidates you may see one really damaging letter. You see it most often in applications for graduate school. A letter will say, "this person is 80 percent great" when you are not looking for 80 percent. It is pretty rare. Most of the time they are enthusiastic. Sometimes they exaggerate, but that is an understandable flaw. Really damaging letters really shouldn't be sent. It is the responsibility of the recommender who has lost faith in a student to find a way out of writing. It is really wrong to write a letter that will hurt someone's career.

Returning to your earlier point about the "elevator" version of the project, my sense is that applicants think they need to be densely technical in their description when something like the complete opposite is the case. Is that so?

More or less. Lamont's study shows that historians generally do better than scholars in many other fields in terms of the number of them that get funding. Among all the humanists and soft social scientists, they tend to be the least technical, and many tell a good story. If there is an important technical point, you need to show mastery of it. But you have to explain it in a nontechnical way. Think about a job talk. The reason you are in that room is because nobody else in that room knows what you are talking about. People attending job talks are mostly tired because it is 4:30 in the afternoon. They are thinking about how to get their kid from daycare. Some of them are Americanists, others are specialists in something else. And if you are talking about the Renaissance in Europe, as many of my students do, they want something that they can follow. You have to speak slowly enough so they'll understand—not so slowly that it's like a dirge. You need to be clear. My wonderful department chair Bill Jordan likes to tell stories, and there's one he told about a job candidate who got up and said, "My name is . . ." and then looked down at his text to remind himself what his name was. He was a very smart person, but he just was not ready to be teaching.

Younger scholars often struggle to discuss theory in their proposals and scholarship. What advice do you have for them?

Theory is something I took on board in the theory years. It helped me in all kinds of ways. There were assumptions about gender, race, class, and culture that I may have brought to my teaching, but that, with the help of theory, I changed. Theory has also made us more critical of our sources than we were before the years when the big debates flared. That said, it seems to me that historians should read enough and think enough about theory that it is useful to them. They should not say what my brilliant late colleague Mark Kishlansky said: "I waited out Foucault, and now I'm waiting out Bourdieu." You should say something to indicate you have done some thinking and reading in theoretical literature and are conscious of it. If, in a job talk, someone in your audience is irritated by any mention of theory, your response should be something like, "I take your point. This is the way I approach this, and we will have to agree to disagree here."

One other thing I'll say, and it is a slightly awkward point, is that there is a certain way of presenting yourself that is most effective for grants, but is less effective for jobs. Particularly when it comes to interdisciplinarity. Societies of fellows and foundations often favor people who, as in *Ghostbusters*, "cross the streams." The selection committee is interdisciplinary, and they want people who can make connections across disciplines. Departments are often looking for something different. They want someone they can recognize as working within their discipline. I'm not saying that a genuinely interdisciplinary scholar should fake being narrow and conventional. But you should present yourself somewhat differently, in a way that shows that you can handle the department's teaching and advising needs. You should not be dishonest in the way you present your work. But rhetoric is all about the audience, and you need to be sensitive to that.

Are there ways in which people often disqualify themselves from grant and fellowship competitions?

In the case of postdocs, many fail at the interview stage. Many if not most postdocs require interviews. The easiest candidates to disqualify are those who give the impression of being obsessively interested in a small technical area. How is he or she going to interact with the rest of the cohort of fellows? How will he or she integrate the younger fellows into the program? Do they interact well with the older people? If all you can talk about is the subject of your dissertation, you won't convince people to take you into a group meant to foster lively conversations and broad teaching. This can be a real problem. Graduate training is very narrowing. You see it with undergrads, the talented ones with wide interests, who make great, unexpected analogies and are fearless about pulling ideas from everywhere. Graduate students, as they are finishing, can be terrified to step outside the box. That is exactly how not to get chosen as one of the five new members of a society of fellows.

One of the reasons I found your essays so compelling when I was thinking about graduate school in history is that they made history more elegant, engaging, and aesthetically pleasing than I knew it to be. What do you tell younger scholars about literary craft?

It is very hard work. I really push my students. Writing is a craft, and as such, you can teach it. I am not a naturally gifted carpenter, but I was well taught and now I am a pretty good carpenter. Similarly, I had no natural gifts as a writer, but I was taught to build a good, solid sentence and paragraph. I want my writing to be as simple, solid, and attractive as it can be. Certain rules help with that. Parallel clauses make people happy. People don't know why they make them happy, but they do. Gibbon was a master of the parallel clause. My colleague David Cannadine coins them effort-lessly. I always push graduate students to use the exact word. To use meta-phors and analogies, to express themselves crisply and precisely. A number of my students have gone from writing as if they were in a defensive crouch, to writing in a bold and effective way.

How do you coach graduate students through failure?

By being as encouraging and supportive as I can, by being in touch regu-larly, [by] responding quickly, and [by] pushing people to come in and talk when times are hard. The biggest single thing students need to know is that the number of bright, energetic, and original early career scholars is much larger than the number of grants that they can apply for, Students—who have succeeded at everything—need to come to terms with the fact that most applications in our field are turned down. At a school like Princeton, where I teach, students have amazing colleagues in each cohort. But they need to realize that there are amazing cohorts else-where too. And they are all really hungry. When I was president of the AHA, and particularly when I was on the council of the AHA for six years, I was impressed by the job sessions. I have been tremendously impressed by all my campus visits. There are amazing numbers of excellent graduate students across the country.

At the same time, it is unnerving to note how many jobs are filled by a small group of some eight departments. There was a big article in Inside Higher Education, and another one in Slate, on a quantitative study that re-vealed the structure of hiring in history in other fields. A group of elite departments controls a huge amount of the market.

What do you tell people in programs other than those top eight?

I asked a female barista at a Starbuck's in Pasadena for a tall blond. She said, I'd like one too, but you've got to be realistic in life. If you look at my field, the one I know best, several of the most important scholars did not get their Ph.D.'s at the top programs. Two of the real stars got their doctorates at Bryn Mawr and Kansas. It is clearly possible to become a major faculty member at a good school if you have a Ph.D. that is not from one of the top places. But you have to work even harder. You have to push yourself hard, and push your advisers hard. You have to have the highest expectations of yourself. And you need publications. People think that conferences are important, but you already get lots of time in front of an audience as a teacher. For me what really makes a dossier is refereed articles. You need real focus and dedication. It's also true that it's hard for people from top institutions too. People don't just sail into jobs and grants, however glittering their qualifications.

Chapter 18

STEPHEN GREENBLATT

Stephen Greenblatt, John Cogan University Professor of the Humanities at Harvard University, is the author of twelve books, including *The Swerve: How the World Became Modern; Shakespeare's Freedom; Will in the World: How Shakespeare Became Shakespeare; Hamlet in Purgatory; Marvelous Possessions;* and *Renaissance Self-Fashioning*. He is general editor of *The Norton Anthology of English Literature* and *The Norton Shakespeare*, has edited seven collections of criticism, and is a founding editor of the journal *Representations*. His honors include the 2012 Pulitzer Prize and the 2011 National Book Award for *The Swerve*, the Modern Language Association's James Russell Lowell Prize (twice), Harvard University's Cabot Fellowship, the Distinguished Humanist Award from the Mellon Foundation, Yale University's Wilbur Cross Medal, the William Shakespeare Award for Classical Theatre, the Erasmus Institute Prize, two Guggenheim fellowships, and the Distinguished Teaching Award from the University of California, Berkeley. He was president of the Modern Language Association of America and is a permanent fellow of the Institute for Advanced Study in Berlin. He has been elected to membership in the American Academy of Arts and Sciences, the American Academy of Letters, and the American Philosophical Society.[1]

What role have grants and fellowships played in your career?

At Berkeley, when I was starting out, there was an office to support faculty research projects. I went through three long three-ring binders and patiently took notes on all the fellowships that were available. Now it is easier. You can find that information online. Second, I went through the research journals in my field, particularly *PMLA*, the *Renaissance Quarterly*, and the *Shakespeare Journal*, looking for announcements of fellowships. Third, I asked around among people in my field what fellowships were available. I tended not to ask senior professors in my department, because I didn't want them to know if I was turned down. So I asked people in my age cohort. They often told me about things that I hadn't heard of. A key point is that as a younger scholar, you shouldn't hope to go sailing into, say, a Guggenheim fellowship. It is technically not out of the question, but it is extremely unlikely to go to people just starting out, because evaluators are told to assess not only the proposal, but the whole career of the applicant. Now there are ACLS Burckhardt fellowships for younger faculty, which is a wonderful idea. Those did not exist when I was a junior faculty member. At the beginning of my career I had a number of very small fellowships. At the time, tiny though they were, they made a huge difference to me.

It often seems that people who get fellowships tend to get more fellowships.

Sometimes that is true. It is the academic "Matthew Principle": to those to whom much is given, more is given.

What are the qualities of an excellent proposal in literary studies?

There are a couple of general measures of intellectual quality in the humanities. We generally do not use proxy indicators like the amount of grant money that has already been awarded. At the same time, we can't simply use the ineffability principle: "I know it when I see it." There have to be some guidelines for judgment. So, for example, there has to be a real problem the project is trying to solve. Also, evaluators ask, can the person explain why this is a significant problem? There are many dimensions to significance. You can apply the "What's the point?" principle. Or the "What difference does it make?" principle. You look for something with insights that you can build on and that might matter to others in the humanities.

Then there are the obvious standards of scholarly quality. There needs to be clarity of expression, rigor in argument, familiarity with sources, a sense of fairness. Honesty and civility toward rival views are important. So is care in citation and fidelity to sources. So is an obvious mastery of methods and the required languages. Those are the basic things you need to be a scholar.

Applicants need to take a critical stance, especially in fields like mine where there is rarely a new discovery being made. Novelty comes in the interpretation. People need to be willing to take on complexity and ambiguity. Reviewers look for originality. That doesn't mean startling newness. A new book or article on *Don Quixote* or *Hamlet* is not going to be absolutely original. But people need to bring new answers to old questions, or new approaches to old questions that cast them in a different light.

What advice do you have for literary scholars on the handling of theory?

I have nothing striking to say on that. Simply invoking theorists, whoever they may be, is not going to win you points. It is worth citing theory if it is relevant and does something important for your argument. But if it is not part of your argument, and is just sort of an add-on, that won't do anything at all. It is also true that at the moment, literary theory is hardly on everyone's lips. People are more worried about how to keep the humanities alive.

One scholar I've spoken with said that the complexity of the theoretical language that was in vogue in the 1980s and 1990s broke public trust in humanistic scholarship. Is that right?

If theory is worth anything to begin with, it can be put in ways that people can understand it. True, Kantians, say, talk to other Kantians in a sort of shorthand, because they share knowledge of the issues they are talking about. But if you are writing for a larger group, you need to be able to explain what the stakes are in the theory you are using.

You need to work from knowledge of whom you are writing for. I wrote a great deal in academic books and articles about Shakespeare's theater as an artisanal production linked to aristocratic hegemony. When I wrote a popular biography of Shakespeare, I did not use this language. I wrote about what it was like to be a carpenter in the Globe Theater. I have friends and students who feel like they have to hold their nose when writing for a larger public, but I think this is a major mistake. Once you start to think you are talking down to the public, you've already lost the game.

I've been struck by how important high-quality writing is in the grant-application process. Do you have any advice on that score?

The intuition that writing is important is a good one. You need to attend to the quality of your writing and also its impact on the reader, emotional or otherwise. It is a bit like Molière's Monsieur Jourdain realizing that he has been speaking in prose all his life. I always try to tell graduate students that they are writers, and should think about themselves as writers. There's something comical about people in English departments not getting that they are writing, and not worrying about the quality of their writing.

Is it important to try to speak to the reader's emotions or pluck the reader's heartstrings?

If it seems like you are conniving to pluck the reader's heartstrings, it ends up sounding like bad Dickens. And I say that as someone who likes Dickens! Your writing can only be moving if it is moving to you.

What do you tell graduate students about the competitiveness of the grant-writing enterprise?

Of course it is competitive! You are talking about money! A lot of people want it. It seems funny not to get that. Everyone gets turned down for everything—for grants, for jobs, for publications. When I was starting out at Berkeley, one of the most respected scholars in my department was a senior professor named Jonas Barish. I told him there was an article of his I read that I thought was terrific. He told me it had been turned down by multiple journals. It was good to know that. I never imagined something like that could be turned down.

Chapter 19

MICHÈLE LAMONT

Michèle Lamont, Robert I. Goldman Professor of European Studies, Harvard University, is a cultural sociologist who studies inequality, race and ethnicity, the evaluation of social science knowledge, and the impact of neoliberalism on advanced industrial societies. Her scholarly interests center on shared concepts of worth and excellence and their impact on hierarchies in a number of social domains. She has written on topics such as how the meanings given to worth (including moral worth) shape ethno-racial and class inequality; the definitions and determinants of societal excellence; and the evaluation of excellence in higher education. Other areas of interest include group boundaries, how members of stigmatized groups respond to racism and discrimination, how culture matters for poverty, peer review, shared criteria of evaluation for qualitative social sciences, disciplinary cultures, and interdisciplinarity.

A past chair of the Council for European Studies, Lamont served as the 108th president of the American Sociological Association. She was elected as a member of the Royal Society of Canada in 2015. She is also the author of *Money, Morals, and Manners: The Culture of the French and the American Upper-Middle Class* (1992), *The Dignity of Working Men: Morality and the*

Boundaries of Race, Class, and Immigration (2000), and *How Professors Think: Inside the Curious World of Academic Judgment* (2009). Her books have won several awards, including the 2002 C. Wright Mills Award from the Society for the Study of Social Problems for *The Dignity of Working Men.*[1]

Lamont has also published more than a hundred peer-reviewed articles and book chapters and has led multiyear collaborative projects that have resulted in collective books: *Rethinking Comparative Cultural Sociology: Repertoires of Evaluation in France in the United States* (with Laurent Thévenot, 2000), *Successful Societies: How Institutions and Culture Affect Health* (with Peter A. Hall, 2009), and *Social Resilience in the Neoliberal Era* (with Peter A. Hall, 2013). Other edited publications include *Workshop on Interdisciplinary Standards for Systematic Qualitative Research* (with Patricia White, 2008).[2]

What advice do you have for younger scholars seeking funding for their research?

If you look at the chapter of *How Professors Think* that deals with criteria of evaluation, two of those criteria really stayed with me. The first is that clarity is absolutely essential. Typically, reviewers have to go through proposals back to back, one after another, and by the end of the day they are very tired. They often de-select more than they select. They are looking for reasons to eliminate proposals. For that reason, the proposal really has to be limpid. It has to have focus. You have to improve the proposal and clarify the central claims, often far more than one would think. It is really important to stick to it and polish the proposal until it is perfect. That can be extremely time-consuming. The more you do it, the better you get at it. One of the characteristics that separates winning proposals from others is the degree to which writers are willing to do the painful and not very interesting work of polishing the prose. Often people will state their argument twice. They state the argument, and then write "in other words. . . ." That is because they are not satisfied with their original statement. They should go back and say it clearly the first time.

The second criterion each applicant needs to focus on is how well he or she establishes the connection between theory and data. When we train graduate students, advisers often need to explain to doctoral students that they may be interested in questions that are impossible to answer, because there are no data available to answer them. Applicants for grants at all levels need to ask: what questions are my data best suited to answer? What can

I show with the data I have? The ability to make connections between theory and data is a skill that develops with time. In that also, you get better at it the more you do it. For accomplished researchers, making those connections is like a fish swimming in water. They are in their element. Younger researchers should take the time to attend a lot of talks by top researchers to see people deploying those skills. This will help them become more accurate and interesting in the way they talk about their own research.

Here is something related to that: the importance of having intellectual range. You have to have access to a broad intellectual toolkit in order to imagine new questions. If you don't, you are handicapped in the grant-application process and much else. You may not be able to draw connections because you haven't read very much. Reading widely in your field and those contiguous to it helps you acquire theoretical literacy and disciplinary literacy. If you have that kind of range, your work is more likely to be original. The most productive people are in conversation with many people, both in their own field and other fields—even those relatively remote from their own.

On the question of productivity, both for people in the social sciences and the humanities: collaboration is very important. It gives you deadlines. Deadlines make you more productive. People often make the mistake of working alone. When they do so, they lose momentum and get lost in their research. That "lost" quality is often visible in the quality of the proposal itself. It undermines the proposal in the sense that it makes the proposal seem less feasible. Feasibility is central to the process of evaluation. Conversely, when people have collaborated with others in their field, and have published abundantly, in the eyes of evaluators, it increases the likelihood that the project will be completed. Past productivity speaks to the applicant's preparation. If someone has never done an ambitious project before, they are often not viewed as capable of doing such a project in the future. Their vita gives evaluators an idea of what they are capable of doing.

Another piece of advice I give younger scholars is try, try, try. People who don't apply don't get anything. To exclude yourself is not smart. But look closely at what the reviewers are saying when you get feedback. Be teachable. Respond thoughtfully to the advice you've been given. This is a crucial asset.

You mentioned connecting theory with data a moment ago. That often trips up younger scholars. What advice do you have for them on that score?

In *How Professors Think*, I described this as an evanescent criterion. Reviewers often don't receive any direction in applying this standard and what it means varies enormously across the disciplines. There is a very good paper by Camic and Gross in the *Annual Review of Sociology* on eight different understandings of theory. Some are most relevant for the humanities, like critical theory à la the Frankfurt School, which is very different from Mertonian middle-range theory, which is more often used in the social sciences.[3] Many of the panelists in literary studies I talked with said there is too much theory used in literary criticism. But theory in that context means something very different from what it means in sociology. I think the question should be addressed differently for each field. For sociology, I like to say that researchers should draw on two sets of literature. One is the literature that gives them analytical tools and concepts—a conceptual frame, such as cultural capital, boundaries, narrative, or social structure. The other literature forms the conversations to which you want to contribute, the questions others have addressed which you also want to consider. What causes inequality? This is an old question that many researchers are working on today. There are many competing hypotheses. For the kind of work I do, you want to have a theoretical focus that is very clear and very well-informed. It cannot just be descriptive. In most fields, purely descriptive work does not count as interesting. If you are looking at social processes, how are certain outcomes enabled by the environment? In *Getting Respect: Dealing with Stigma and Discrimination in the United States, Brazil, and Israel* (2016), our explanatory approach is configurational: i.e., about macro- and meso-level factors that enable and constrain patterns in the way given groups and individuals respond to other groups and individuals. It is very different from variable-based analysis that privileges replicability.[4] But the way scholars respond to theory varies enormously from field to field. To return to my earlier point: many literary critics are skeptical of proposals that seem to rely too heavily on theory. Sophisticated literary scholars often hesitate over proposals in which theory is mentioned just to position oneself and to signal where one belongs. Are you Foucauldian or Judith Butlerian? People say there is too much symbolic use of theory. The larger point is that different disciplines require different approaches to theory.

Since readers of grant proposals are often not from the applicant's field, does that mean they have to translate theories from their discipline for outsiders?

One way to answer that is that historians win grants in larger proportion because they write much better. The work they do appeals more easily to interdisciplinary evaluators. They speak convincingly about the significance of the work. It is normally the job of the evaluator not to dismiss the work because they don't get it. People who serve on these committees have to have the intellectual breadth to understand proposals from multiple disciplinary perspectives. But not all competitions are of equal quality. When panelists use idiosyncratic criteria to evaluate proposals, you need a program officer or another panelist to stand up to them and say, "No, that is not a valid objection." But this does not always happen, of course.

I was very interested in your analysis of literary studies, and the difficulty that literary scholars have in agreeing on criteria of evaluation. Given that, what do you advise applicants from literary fields to do?

I think if you ask a literary scholar they would say that there are criteria. They would say those criteria would have to do with clarity and the quality of the writing. They would say the criteria have to do with the extent to which applicants are steeped in the relevant knowledge and have command of the crucial debates in the discipline, and the whole range of positions people are taking. Saying something original is crucial. Literary scholars have at least four or five criteria by which they evaluate proposals. Now, how does that manifest itself concretely? There are variations. Two scholars would react to a given proposal very differently. My answer is that many practitioners who are very involved in the evaluation of literary criticism would believe there are criteria.

Do you think there are criteria?

Yes, I do. If you study a competition and several people make the same comments on a given proposal, there are criteria for the evaluation of literary criticism. If there is 80 percent convergence among the evaluators, there are criteria that they share. Other fields may have a convergence of only 40 percent. As I argue in Chapter 2 of *How Professors Think*, evaluative cultures vary a lot across fields.

It sounds like convergence among reviewers is key to determining whether they are using valid criteria.

My position would be that there are no intrinsically valid criteria. Instead, we find subjective agreement on the importance of some criteria. The way it works is that evaluators typically rank the candidates before the meeting and the grant-making institution compiles the rankings and distributes them to the reviewers at the start of the face-to-face deliberations. It often happens that more than one reviewer will give candidates the same ranking. That convinces program officers and panelists that there is convergence. Once convergence happens, it convinces people that excellence actually exists. One thing that complicates that, though, is there is a tendency to downplay differences after a group of evaluators identifies consensus over a given proposal.

I was struck by the consensus-driven quality of these decisions. That is not the case with other decisions in academia, like those over tenure and promotion, for instance.

Tenure is different. There are considerations in tenure processes that do not pertain to the quality of the work. For instance, tenure can alter the balance of power and the relative salience of areas of specialization within the department. If you give tenure to a Europeanist, what does that mean for the Latin American program? There are competitions for hegemony within each department and each tenure decision influences that. If it is an ecology where people make many decisions together, each decision is not independent from the others. On the contrary, each decision is dependent on all the others in complicated ways. Some people may feel they are always on the losing side, and that affects their ability to make arguments that can persuade their colleagues. People always say that with tenure, the good cases are easy and the bad cases are easy. It is the cases in the middle that are hard. Cases in which competing criteria are used are the most difficult. You get different evaluations of the same product depending on the criteria that are used.

In reading How Professors Think, I was struck by your critique of Bourdieu, and your argument that decisions about grants are made not to further an agenda or consolidate power, but out of civic-mindedness.

The kinds of organizations I study are very prestigious—the American Council of Learned Societies, for instance. Of course, people are happy to serve as panelists in ACLS competitions, because it gives them a chance to influence the distribution of resources in their field and across the academy. But they also agree to serve on such panels because they are honored to be asked, or because they have received funding and want to give back to funders that have supported their work in the past. That is very different from serving on a promotion committee, which is more of a service to your department.

Have the priorities of grant-making institutions changed over time, or has the pursuit of excellence remained something of a fixed star for them?

Disciplines diffuse different visions of excellence. In disciplines where Foucault has been influential, scholars think about excellence as something that is constructed and institutionalized, an epistemic discourse of a sort. In contrast, in economics, though they are familiar with the Kuhnian notion of the paradigm shift, they tend to essentialize excellence. People at the top of their fields tend to think there is something objective about excellence. That may have to do at least in part with age and generational culture. In more scientist fields, scholars are more likely to think there are objective standards of excellence. In fields where postmodernism is influential, that is not the case.

There are also differences between the ways that public and private institutions operate. At the University of Texas at Austin, where I taught at the start of my career, the university was much more proactive in overseeing scholarly activity than Harvard University is. At the University of California, Los Angeles, the university is very much in the service of California. That drives many of the choices the administration makes. That is less of a concern at private institutions.

Across the academy, diversity is more salient now than it was twenty years ago. Also, all data show that academics are working longer hours than they ever did before. They are all overburdened. Our lives are very different from that of the gentleman academic of long ago. Work conditions are different. Even the social origins of faculty members are different. There are more dual-career families now. I remember that when I arrived at Princeton University in 1987, I was told that social life among the faculty had been transformed drastically after faculty spouses started working. There were far fewer dinner parties, because both husbands and wives were working. That brought about a huge change in what it meant to be a faculty member. A world of genteel cocktail parties is less likely when you were raising toddlers and you have two young professionals working fifty hours a week.

One person I spoke with said he thought the consensus-driven nature of the process made it difficult for truly original work to get funded. He argued that, in political science, for instance, the triumph of rational choice has been so thorough that it has become hegemonic and excludes alternative approaches.

I am not sure I agree. Rational choice is much less hegemonic now than it was fifteen years ago. Many would say that paradigm is losing speed, with the cognitive revolution in economics and other fields. Behavioral economics is destroying many of the assumptions on which economics used to be based. That landscape is very much changed. As the economy itself has changed, macroeconomic theory and labor economics have changed with it. Political science is also going through a phase where everyone is concerned with counterfactual and value-controlled experiments. But new books, like *Advances in Comparative-Historical Analysis* by James Mahoney and Kathleen Thelen, have come out that are critical of that and argue that this trend toward methodological purity is leading to a narrowing and impoverishment of the field.[5]

So, from where I sit, the state of these fields seems quite dynamic. True, there are committees where you find different trends, perhaps at the National Science Foundation (NSF). I led a committee for the NSF on evaluating the quality of research in the social sciences. Consistent with the influence of King, Keohane, and Verba's *Designing Social Inquiry*, some political scientists argued that qualitative research in their field should meet the standards to which quantitative research is held.[6] I don't think this is wise. If replicability is given more weight as a criterion of judgment, you are setting up qualitative research for a losing battle. Qualitative and quantitative research projects should play on an even field, and those evaluating qualitative projects should consider under what light qualitative research shines, and what it is uniquely good for. This subordination of qualitative to quantitative research in political science has led some political scientists to use sociology as a new point of reference.

Speaking more generally, I always put my money on the fact that people get tired of closing off options. Young people will always want to make their reputation by trying out some new approach or set of questions.

Chapter 20

MICHAEL C. MUNGER

Michael C. Munger, professor of political science at Duke University, received his Ph.D. in economics at Washington University in St. Louis in 1984. Following his graduate training, he worked as a staff economist at the Federal Trade Commission. His first teaching job was in the Economics Department at Dartmouth College; later he took on appointments in the Political Science Department at the University of Texas at Austin (1986–1990) and the University of North Carolina at Chapel Hill (1990–1997). At UNC he directed the Master of Public Administration Program, which trains public-service professionals, especially in city and county management.

He moved to Duke University in 1997 and served as chair of the Political Science Department from 2000 through 2010. He has won three university-wide teaching awards (the Howard Johnson Award, an NAACP "Image" Award for teaching about race, and admission to the Bass Society of Teaching Fellows). He is currently director of Duke's interdisciplinary Philosophy, Politics, and Economics Program.

Munger's research interests include the study of the morality of exchange and the working of legislative institutions in producing policy. Much of his recent work has been in philosophy, examining the concept of truly voluntary exchange, a concept for which he coined the term "euvoluntary." He has created a new blog devoted to investigating examples of, and controversies about, euvoluntary exchange. His primary blog, Kids Prefer Cheese, is an irreverent look at policy, politics, and the foibles of pundits everywhere.[1]

What role have grants and fellowships played in your career?

In the earlier part of my career I moved around a bit. For a while I was an administrator at the University of North Carolina. I was the dean of a very small program, a master's of public administration, in essence. It was a professional program. We depended quite a lot on clients. I was not used to thinking that way. I was trained as an economist, and later worked at the U.S. Federal Trade Commission. At the FTC, our idea was we would do analyses and the world was supposed to look at what we did and then change its mind. You publish your research and you make an impact. We soon found out that was not the case. It was like throwing a stone down a well. Maybe five minutes later you hear a distant little plink when it hits the bottom. Working for clients is interesting. It's different. At UNC, we got some small grants for students. We got some others for faculty. All the students were supposed to have a client in mind when they applied for grant money. That changed my views a little bit compared to what I had been doing. That is typical of young people.

By chance I was later invited to participate on a National Science Foundation panel. It was a group of six political scientists who convene twice a year after the submission date to make judgments on seventy to seventy-five proposals. We could fund five of them. There would also be applications that students submitted for dissertation-improvement grants. I was struck by how bad the proposals were. And I was thunderstruck to realize that my proposals were just as bad. I was amazed to find that the problem was not that of narrowing down a highly competitive pool to five or six, but rather to find five proposals that were worth funding.

Why were the proposals so bad?

In applying for grants it's all about how not to fail. You have to fail to fail, and you'll have a decent chance of funding. That's why I came up with a visual image for graduate students. Students think that the reviewer finishes her busy work for the morning, gets a fresh cup of tea, opens the window to let in the bright cheery morning, and then sits down to spend two leisurely hours studying this proposal. That's not true.

Instead, the student needs to imagine that it's 5:30 a.m., and the reviewer is on some crappy exercise bike in a hotel "fitness room." She is pretty angry, because she has a stack of seven proposals to look through in the next ninety minutes. She is mostly looking for a reason to turn proposals down quickly, because if the proposal is good she'll have to spend much more time on it. And she can't spend a lot of time on more than two or three of the seven, since only one of them is likely to get funded in this round.

Most potential applicants make this easy, though, by omitting or disguising basic information such as the main question, alternative hypotheses, the main dependent variable, the method, the form of the data being collected, or the likely deliverables. Successful PIs [primary investigators] make it much harder to turn the proposal down, because they highlight all those things in simple language, and explain what's at stake. What will be done with the money, and why is this project worth funding more than the others? Everybody wants money to go think about what they will do. Projects that are clear and where the PI has thought things through are much harder to turn down.

I find this mental image of the wretched person on the exercise bike versus the happy person with a fresh cup of tea really helps the students understand who their immediate audience is.

For those of us who are not social scientists, can you explain a "dependent variable"?

It is usually a puzzle. What is the puzzle you are working on? What would make the world a better place if you had an explanation for it? It is the thing you are trying to explain. I've often read proposals and I would have no clue what that dependent variable is, and I'd throw it away. It is easy to throw away proposals that fail to communicate that, or that fail to communicate excitement, or what is at stake. It's easy to discard proposals that don't say clearly why you should fund this project and not something else. When you are writing your proposal, think about that angry person on the exercise bike, not someone who is immediately disposed to agree with you. You have to have a section early in the proposal that identifies that independent variable. It is simpler than explaining it; you have to identify it. There will be six to eight people reading your proposal, and for you to have a chance, someone on that committee has to be your champion. You have to make it easy for that person to find what it is you are trying to explain. It should be in bold letters, such that your champion can say, "Look, here it is on page three." That is what will get you into the final ten proposals. Maybe not into the circle of winners, but into the final round.

Once you're in that final round, how do you separate the excellent from the merely very good?

It is not easy. Something like fifty of the seventy proposals will have nothing in them about what is at stake, what the data are, what the dependent variable is. You can study the proposals long and hard and still not find out. The process of evaluation is not what I thought it was originally. I spent hours trying to explain my research to someone who was already interested in it. It was full of incredibly opaque prose. It was almost encrypted. You have to show what you are going to do, and why I should care. It's true that ultimately you are appealing to specialists. They will push your proposal, and try to sell it to others with different specialties. But there are others who are trying to shoot it down and get funding for their area. Even if you are speaking to specialists on the committee, remember, they are tired. Make it possible for those specialists to explain your work to others on the committee.

One of the big things I always tell graduate students about, because almost all of them make this mistake[, is that] the core of what they are trying to accomplish is wrong. They're saying, "I am really smart. Here's what I've done. Give me money to think about this." It never works. Stupid but clear proposals will always win and get funded. Proof by forward reference works. If you say you intend to do a survey with randomized trials, and there are thirty interviews with people that were done as part of a pilot project, and here is the scientific deliverable, that is going to be effective. You have to be clear on what you will use the money for.

It seems like there is a premium on exactitude in describing how the money will be spent.

Yes. For instance, you can get a letter from the survey company you are going to use. In my discipline there has been a scandal over Michael LaCour, a graduate student at Berkeley who published an article in *Science* that turned out to have been based on fabricated data. I wrote on this in the *Chronicle of Higher Education*. You can get a letter from the survey company you want to use. It is easy to get. You can show that you got a bid, the company has done this before and can do it again. It takes about a half an hour. The fact that LaCour did not have that letter was a real red flag. No graduate students do it though, and they should. Because they don't want to think about the deliverable. The measure of success of a grant proposal is to show that you can conceive and execute a research plan. Graduate students try to show this is not true by not committing to anything and keeping it vague. They do not want to be tied down. But that is not the nature of the game. You don't get to make the rules of the game. You just want to win. And because it is a game, losing is not personal. Graduate students ask me, "What if I don't get funded?" That is completely normal. You should think of the first three times you submit your grant proposal as practice.

Boring and specific always gets funding faster than interesting and vague. That is true across the board. For every funding agency. Except Mac-Arthur "genius" grants. That kind of makes the point. They say you are so smart, here is a grant and do what you will. Nobody else does that.

How do you help students cope with the high rate of failure in grant applications?

Grants allow you to have time off from teaching. If it's a government grant, it comes with overhead for the university. It confers prestige. The competition is fierce. Why do you think you are God's special snowflake? For the graduate students at elite universities, they have been winners all their lives. Now you are competing in a much more competitive game, and you have to recognize that you will learn from the process.

I use a technical metaphor for this. If you are writing a computer program in HTML, you don't stare at the code to see if it is all correct. You submit it to the computer to see if it comes back with error messages. You don't sit there staring at the code. You should think of proposals the same way. Even if you don't think it's perfect, submit it and see what comes back. There are limits to that. It can't be embarrassing. But if it is not embarrassing, submit it. The committee is a group of smart people who are working as your unpaid research assistants. If they criticize the proposal, it hurts. But they're right. If, as I said, you fail to fail, their comments are likely to be substantive. If you follow their advice, you are more likely to have a better project and to get more money later for their having turned it down.

It seems like most applicants don't realize they can get the readers' comments after the fact.

Yes. But you can also get comments *before* the fact, depending on the agency. Most of the research money I get is from foundations. The biggest indicator determining success in applying to them—it dwarfs all the others—is did the person meet with the program office before submitting the proposal? If you contact the program officers, you can ask them what the foundation is interested in. [They are] not like journal referees. They want good proposals. They want to spend their money on good projects, and the program officers partly get credit for funding programs that the foundation is interested in. Doing this involves some cold calling. I recently got three million dollars from the NEH. But that was after I met four times with the program officer. He knew the proposal was coming, and knew it responded to his agency's interests. It is not cheating to contact the program office. Students think it is, but it is not cheating. The interest of the program officer is to improve the quality of the proposals his agency receives. It has gotten so that foundations sometimes contact me and ask if I could use another $100,000. I say yes, we could. We can hire two more postdocs with that. It's because they sometimes do not get enough high-quality proposals, and they want to spend their money effectively.

What kinds of changes have you observed in the world of grant making over your career?

It has changed in three ways. If you talk to an officer at the NSF, they will give you guarded comments on the changes in the agency's interests. But the first big change has been that it has gotten harder to get grants with overhead, and those are the ones that really count at universities. That's true with the NSF, the NEH, the IAS [Institute for Advanced Study], and others. Those grants with large overhead were the bread and butter of research universities. Now it is very hard to get those grants for all but the very top places. The second big change is that universities value that kind of funding more than ever before. It is a bigger part of the third-year review, tenure review, and post-tenure review than ever before. It counts a lot, particularly at state universities. It counts more than you may expect when it comes to support from the administration. If you have participated in fundraising, it has more weight than you think.

The third big change has been the increasing importance of foundations. Some foundations are interested in particular areas of politics or policy, whether it be education, homelessness, poverty, or child nutrition. There has been a huge proliferation of private foundations that young people don't think about enough. You have to cultivate a relationship with them. They generally won't take a proposal over the transom. You have to talk with the program officer, and maybe three years down the line you are likely to get something. Another thing about them is that if you have gotten a grant from them, they are likely to sign up with you again. If you come back to them and propose to continue a project they have funded, they are likely to go along with it.

It sounds like inequality may have something to do with this.

It does. There are a lot of rich people out there. They say, "Wow, did I ever make a lot of money. Now I'd like to give back." Melinda Gates went to Duke. She has been a big benefactor to Duke. The Bill and Melinda Gates Foundation has invested heavily in Duke. So yes, there are a lot of rich people out there, but now they want to spend their money on things they think will help people. You could call it inequality. Or you could call it the consequence of the concentration of wealth in fewer hands.

Returning to an earlier comment, how does one go about cultivating a relationship with a foundation?

There is no generic answer. Foundations are very specialized. Some work in health policy, for instance. You should talk with senior people about what funds what sort of work. If you are in English literature, there are funds interested in promoting education in the humanities. If you are at a small liberal arts college, you can get a grant for $10,000 a year to fund a speaker series. That will be a gigantic benefit to the college. You can run a real speaker series with that. People in the development office need two more zeros behind that to take notice. They will try to block your getting that grant. They want control over how we get money. I've found myself in trouble after I approached a foundation. But now, I don't submit my grant proposals to the development office until after I have come to agreement with the foundation. There is an element of sales in this kind of work. You call five foundations, and they may not get back to you. But you only need one. You say what you're interested in—maybe to hire a postdoc or hire an adjunct professor. Here's one way to pitch it: you can say there are so many underemployed people, our hiring them to an adjunct position would be a benefit to them, and to our students because nobody we have teaches what this adjunct does. That's the kind of thing foundations want to do. They generally are not interested in providing summer salaries for research. But if there is a position you want to add to teach Jane Austen, because you don't have a course on Austen and you need it, that is something foundations are interested in.

Since different disciplines evaluate quality in different ways, how should grant writers think about writing for a multidisciplinary committee?

One thing to think about is the final product the writer is planning on producing. Is this going to be a database? A series of articles? A book? The problem with books is that they are kind of like federal government grants: they are hard to get. It used to be that if you have a decent manuscript and your adviser recommends it, there is a good chance a press is going to publish it. If they sold seven hundred copies, they used to break even. Now they are looking to sell fifteen hundred copies. It is so hard to get a book published. I have a couple of friends who have tried without success for years. Presses are looking for larger revenues and more impact. Each discipline handles this differently. History is a book discipline. Philosophy is a book discipline. In the Ivy League, political science is a book discipline. Political science departments at the state schools are all focused on articles. So your grant proposal should let the reviewer envision the book or series of articles you [want] to produce. It used to be that you could get a grant to buy you out of a teaching requirement or to get summer support to finish a book. That is still true for some foundations. People should do it more. But you need to cultivate a relationship with the foundation.

What are the some of the common mistakes that grant writers make?

It is human nature for evaluators to think [that] if [they] have published something on the subject and the proposal doesn't cite [them,] it's already not good. Then you go about finding a reason why. People think, "You don't cite me, you bastard!" I've noticed that sometimes in evaluating proposals. People can get pretty angry and they devote effort to thinking of reasons why the proposal is bad, but it's really because the proposal doesn't cite them. So grant writers need to think about other scholars who have written on their topic. Make an effort to find out who has written on it. So many graduate students hold up a round thing and say, "I've invented the wheel!" They think if someone has written about their topic, their own work is less valuable. The opposite is true. If others have written about your topic, it means people think it is important. Graduate students often fail to read scholarship on their topic because they want to be the first to write about it. . . . Part of the problem is that we tell students their dissertation has to be this grand thing that is "Original Scholarship." What that really means is that it is a genuine incremental advance in knowledge on topics that others have worked on.

I was curious about something you mentioned earlier about envisioning the final product. Many funded proposals are going to turn into books, but do proposals that envision an article or series of articles ever get funded?

In the hard sciences that is all there is. In the social sciences and humanities, it is not like that. Funded proposals are generally either for the writing of a series of articles or a book. It helps if you say which of those you are aiming to write. The tradeoff is that a series of articles can seem ambitious but vague. Ambition is a drawback if you are not specific in what you propose. Applicants need to be both ambitious and specific. For historians it is sometimes easier to do that. Some competitions will allow you to include a scanned document as an appendix to the proposal, such that you can say, "This letter refers specifically to another letter that I am looking for." And you can propose to go to the archive where that letter is. That way the reader knows what you are trying to do.

Theory tends to trip up younger scholars. Do you have any advice on that score?

I have an embarrassing admission. At the National Science Foundation, every time I went, I would always bring a sock puppet. It had googly eyes and yarn hair. I bought it at a yard sale. I called him Mr. Theory. Whenever we were discussing a proposal that I did not think addressed theory adequately, Mr. Theory would come out from under the table and say, in a high-pitched voice, "Mr. Theory doesn't like this proposal!" After a while, he would only have to peek up over the edge of the table, and people would know what was coming. The rest of the committee would say, "Okay, okay, we know." Grant proposals don't have to produce an entirely new theory. But candidates need to know what body of theory their work is going to contribute to. In physics, you need to show how an empirical finding has implications for the big theories in the field. In the humanities, people are often looking for a new theory. For a while it tore up English departments. Before that, there were too many dissertations simply on Hamlet. Then it became, "Is Hamlet gay?" People were just coming up with stuff to be provocative. Now literary studies seem to have swung back from that. So yes, theory is important. You need to tie down what theoretical questions you are trying to address. Sometimes you see proposals about things like editing the letters of a fifteen-year-old slave girl as a way of focusing on excluded voices. But proposals like that will not get funded if they don't show how the project will speak to larger theoretical concerns.

In political science there have been two great revolutions, the first one over behaviorism and the second over rational choice. Both of them were bloody. It is difficult to say what the standards of judgment are across the field. If you look at the introductory course syllabi for the top political science programs, there is about 10 percent overlap from one program to the next. They often don't even cover the same topics. Political science is riven by debate over methods, and what counts as truth. Is it mathematical proof? Argumentation? I am an economist, and in economics, theory means math. In political science, theory often means moral philosophy. I get into trouble all the time when I say theory, because it means different things to different people. It is context dependent. But whatever you do, you need to connect your work to some field of normative theory.

I have been interested to hear from the people I've interviewed that despite all these deep disagreements both within and across fields, the grant evaluation process is pretty collegial.

It is collegial generally. I have been chair of the Political Science Department at Duke and I've been editor of two journals. Some evaluation processes are more contentious than others. Tenure decisions are not collegial.

There was a famous case where an argument over tenure devolved into a fistfight. At faculty meetings, people sometimes yell. But at the NSF, it has been very collegial. I've sometimes wondered if it is because it is a self-perpetuating body of people like me who get to choose who to include in the club. It is not clear to me if the lack of acrimonious dissent is a cause or an effect of that.

It sounds a little like a cabal.

In some respects it is, but it is not like we have some smoky room where we convene. In my case, my dissertation committee had members who went on to be the chairs of the economics departments of Harvard and Stanford, and a third member who won the Nobel Prize. It was a big help to my career and had nothing to do with me. In the rational choice debate it was my side that won. Since I was in that club, I was selected to be a member of these grant-making committees, because I will do the right thing. At a larger level, this is how the dominant paradigm protects itself. It is not because we have secret meetings. We are not a cabal in that sense. We don't have to meet. It is totally open. It is possible that truly innovative work is impossible to publish in top journals or will not be funded by top agencies. Revolutions always come from the outside of the established structures. The disciplines are inherently conservative.

Chapter 21

SHERRY SMITH

Sherry Smith's research rests at the intersection of western, Native American, and U.S. cultural history. A University Distinguished Professor and co-director of the Clements Center for Southwest Studies at Southern Methodist University, her most recent books include *Hippies, Indians, and the Fight for Red Power* (2012) and *Reimagining Indians: Native Americans through Anglo Eyes, 1880–1940* (2000), which won the Organization of American Historians' James Rawley Prize for the best book on race relations. She has also published two edited volumes as part of the Clements Center symposia series: *Indians and Energy: Exploitation and Opportunity in the American Southwest* (2010) and *The Future of the Southern Plains* (2003). A former president of the Western History Association (2008–2009), she held the *Los Angeles Times* Distinguished Fellowship at the Huntington Library (2009–2010) and received the Berkshire Prize for Best Article in 2010. Her current research project is a biography of a relationship between two early twentieth-century advocates for free love living on the West Coast.[1]

What experience do you have as both an applicant and evaluator of grant proposals?

I do a lot of evaluating of proposals, not just at the Clements Center, but also for the NEH, Fulbright, and the ACLS. And I have been doing it for quite a few years. As an applicant I have received various NEH grants, grants for research at the Huntington library, and a Fulbright in New Zealand. I've applied for an ACLS but didn't get it. I never submitted an application for a Clements Center fellowship. I was at UTEP [University of Texas at El Paso] when then-director David Weber encouraged me to apply. My response was that I didn't want to live in Dallas! I also am not really a specialist in the Southwest or the borderlands.

What are some of the most common mistakes that grant applicants make?

Great question. For the Clements Center, there is a well-defined mission. The applicant has to make it clear in his application that his project relates to the Southwest (fairly broadly defined), Texas, or the borderlands. We recently added a stipulation that California after 1821 was not considered eligible, reflecting our donor's wishes. His primary purpose in endowing the Clements Center was to enhance scholarship on Texas and the borderlands, understood as New Mexico, Arizona, and Northern Mexico. Applicants must read the guidelines for the fellowship carefully and make sure their project fits the geographical orientation of our program. If their project is bigger and broader, but has a component that is Texas- or borderlands-based, then that can work. So we have some wiggle room. But the project has to meet the donor's expectations and the mission of the Clements Center. Some cases are easy to eliminate simply because they do not fit the center's mission.

The second mistake we often see is that people explain the value of their project as "This has never been done before. It fills a gap in the historiography." That is not sufficient justification. You have to show that the project has a deeper significance and explain why that is so. You can add that nobody has done it before, but that alone will not win a fellowship. The core issue is: does the project convey an important and significant [contribution]? You have to make a substantial contribution beyond simply filling a gap in the literature. Those who do not do that are not as successful.

Do those same principles hold true in the other competitions you've judged?

The Fulbright often has geographical requirements like the Clements Center, but there too, the issue of the project's significance is more important.

How might applicants frame proposals in such a way that they will be appealing across disciplines?

The majority of the Clements Center's successful applicants are historians. But we have also given fellowships to archaeologists, anthropologists, one historian of anthropology, at least one art historian, and literary scholars. In more recent years, we have granted more fellowships to people whose work is interdisciplinary. We have also seen more grants going to historians whose work transcends various subfields of history. If the project is interdisciplinary and it is explained well, that can get them to the top of the pile. There is one I can think of whose work spans Native American [issues], urban history, energy history, and political history. He was juggling four different historiographies and looked at the ways people approached power in the West, both electrical power and political power, as it was contested by whites and Indians, urban and rural groups. It was very rich and multilayered, but not interdisciplinary. It made use of various angles and approaches within the historical discipline. Ethnohistory is another example which incorporates historical and anthropological approaches.

It seems like disciplinary boundaries are becoming less and less important in the grant-making world.

That is less the case in my experience of both the NEH and the ACLS, in which I've only been asked to evaluate the history applications. But within SMU, I have worked on committees that evaluated applicants from all disciplines. When the committee is constituted that way, it is extremely important to be able to explain your work to people outside your discipline. There has to be great clarity in how you explain your work. It has to be in clear, straightforward English and not depend on the jargon of your discipline. One thing I will say is that applications in philosophy drive me crazy. They are working in another world from the other people in the humanities. I never understand what they are saying. The same is true of physics and chemistry, of course. But we tend to give them more of a break and turn to the scientists in the group. In the humanities, there is no excuse for not being able to explain what you are doing to nonspecialists. Historians have an advantage in that our work is fairly easily translated and made comprehensible to nonhistorians. Applicants should be aware that their audience may not know their field.

One task that often trips up applicants is writing about other people's scholarship. What advice do you have for them?

The first piece of advice comes from something Roy Ritchie of the Huntington Library said when he gave a talk at SMU about how to get grants. You have to say what you are doing in the first paragraph. You have to put it right out front, because, unfortunately, many readers won't actually read the whole application. That was a little deflating and discouraging to our graduate students. I do always read the whole application. But people often don't. So do not begin the application with historiography. You have to underscore what you are doing early in the application. You should also include what contribution you are making to the historiography. You don't want to offend readers by ignoring their work, or their friends' work, or the work of people they respect. You have to have a brief summary of the historiography. If you are allowed to have footnotes, put it there. It is sort of a balancing act, demonstrating you know what is out there already. There is no easy answer to this. It is complicated. You have to convey mastery of the field, while not being too fawning, which undermines the value of what you are doing. This discussion should come in the second or third paragraph, and should be authoritative. But it should also emphasize there is more work to be done. Applicants' primary focus must be on what they are doing, and what fresh ideas they bring to the topic.

Theory also presents something of a stumbling block.

It can be. When I was in graduate school we got zero encouragement to engage in theoretical stuff. I have learned the value of it. I don't do a lot of it though. I think some people do it well. To include theory is fine. To overdo it is not good. If you leave it out entirely, that can hurt you. It also depends on who is reading the application. It is interesting: in my many years of evaluating applications, when groups of readers get together, they almost always agree on which applications rise to the top. There are never deep divisions. You always come up with the same ones. To have no theory is not good, but neither is having too much of it. Theory is not absolutely essential. The Clements Center has had very successful fellows who have not had clear grounding in theory. Others integrate theory in a way that really does make their applications more attractive. Some engage theory in a very superficial way in an attempt to look impressive, but it does not enhance the value of their work. You have to be careful. If it comes across as just throwing in theory as an afterthought, that is not helpful.

How do you help younger scholars cope with the high rate of failure in grant applications?

Anyone who is honest has the same experience of frequent failure. I have often thought the leading lights of my field should do a conference panel on their personal failure in grant applications. It would be very helpful for younger scholars to know how often even the best people have failed. You simply have to accept it. It is inevitable. But you can't let it discourage you. You can try to learn from failure. The NEH will give you panelists' comments. They may enrage you. But they can help you when you revise and resubmit your work. It is so important to accept that rejections are just a part of our work. It has gotten so hard to get an NEH grant, for instance. The only thing you can do is view it as part of your professional experience, and to learn from it.

What advice do you have for applicants in their relations with their recommenders?

You need to make sure the person really knows your project, and can speak about its importance in detail. There are a couple of things that applicants really can't control. Two things I've noticed are that sometimes the person who writes the letter produces a much better explanation of the project than the applicant does. It's not that the letter writer is smarter, but they have been at this for a long time. They are more experienced. It doesn't exactly hurt the applicant, but sometimes the recommendation letters give a more cogent explanation of the project than the applicant does. The other thing is that the opposite can sometimes happen. I have read some terrible letters. They are not trying to hurt the applicant. It's just that they are not very good writers. I have to say, the Ivy League recommenders are fabulous. They really have this down. Yale people write great letters. Other people don't write as many letters or perhaps are not as accomplished at it. This does not help applicants. In a sense, recommenders are competing with each other. We do read them all. And we always understand that they are on the side of the applicant. But they need to convince readers. Some faculty need training on how to write a persuasive letter.

What does a bad letter look like?

Well, they need to address the project in detail. A superficial letter, or a poorly written letter, doesn't do that. If the professor does not understand the project and see its value, if they can't articulate why the project is important, that will hurt the applicant. You have to write a substantive letter that conveys something about the project, a really strong, deep, sophisticated explanation of why this is important.

Have you ever seen intentionally damning letters?

They are very rare. I can think of one, where the letter was very short and not positive. Ironically the person still got the fellowship. You would hope a professor would have the integrity to tell the person that he just can't write for him.

Chapter 22

PAULINE YU

Pauline Yu, president of the American Council of Learned Societies since July 2003, also served, from 1994 to 2003, as dean of humanities in the College of Letters and Science and professor of East Asian Studies at the University of California, Los Angeles. Prior to those appointments, she was founding chair of the Department of East Asian Languages and Literature at the University of California, Irvine (1989–1994) and on the faculties of Columbia University (1985–1989) and the University of Minnesota (1976–1985). She received her bachelor of arts degree in history and literature from Harvard University and her master's and Ph.D. in comparative literature from Stanford University. She is the author or editor of five books and dozens of articles on classical Chinese poetry, literary theory, comparative poetics, and issues in the humanities, and has received fellowships from the Guggenheim Foundation, the American Council of Learned Societies, and the National Endowment for the Humanities. She was awarded the William Riley Parker Prize for best *PMLA* article of 2007.[1]

What role have grants and fellowships played in your career, as an applicant, evaluator, and now as head of a large grant-making institution?

I have been awarded fellowships from, among others, ACLS, NEH, Guggenheim, and the Association for American University Women, each of which supported completion of my dissertation or subsequent books. In recent years I haven't had to, primarily because I've been unable to take the time off. I haven't been on a sabbatical since 1983–1984. (My life changed after I became a department chair in 1989.) The more salient piece of information is that I have been on selection panels for a host of organizations for thirty years. A rough estimate of the number of applications I have read is somewhere between two to three thousand.

In your experience, what are the most common mistakes that applicants make?

There are a few of them. One is that you should not take for granted that any reader of your application knows what you are talking about. People often write their applications for a specialist audience, but proposals are likely to be read by an interdisciplinary panel, so you have to be able to speak outside of your field.

A second mistake is a hobbyhorse of mine, which I call "mind the gap." When you say that you are filling an important gap in the literature, that is immediately two strikes against you. If your only argument for your project is that no one has done it before, that is not enough. It may be true, but it is not persuasive. More effective proposals could say something like, "These are the received propositions about this topic, and I am contesting them." You start with a standard explanation of what you are studying, and you show how you've got a different and better one.

Third, you have to have an answer to the "so what?" question. You need to show why your project is significant.

Fourth, a grant proposal should not read like a book proposal. It should have an argument. Some book proposals do that, but many of them are descriptive, saying, "In chapter one I will do X, in chapter two I will do Y," etc. That is not very compelling as a grant proposal. With some proposals, the author's nose is a little too close to the ground.

Some strong applications tell a good story, and that can be very effective. It is almost a cliché to start the proposal with an anecdote, but if it is appropriate, that can work well. You should certainly have a strong lead paragraph.

Over your career have you seen significant changes in the funding priorities of the ACLS and other agencies like it?

Our Central Fellowship Program is open with respect to subject; its priority is simply quality, to fund what the peer-review process judges to be the best scholarship in the humanities. I would say that the range of funded projects is certainly broader and more varied than it was when the program began. Without overlooking the importance of more traditional scholarship, which continues to fare well in the competitions, I think that the projects we fund, not surprisingly, now reflect the increasing diversity of approaches to humanistic research. There has also been a tremendous geographical expansion of topics. Fifty years ago, the vast majority of proposals were focused on the Anglo-American and Mediterranean world; now that is clearly not the case.

Beyond the Central program, we have also, over the years, introduced certain newer fellowships directed to specific career moments: our Burkhardt grants for recently tenured faculty, for instance. We have programs for people working with new methodologies as well, such as digital scholarship and collaborative scholarly projects. We have a program designed to place Ph.D.'s in nonacademic jobs, the Public Fellows program. We've tried to be attentive to changes in the academic landscape of the humanities and are pleased that in many instances other organizations have followed our lead.

ACLS has always been committed to supporting internationally focused scholarship, and we currently have programs in African, Chinese, and Buddhist studies. These, like ones I just mentioned, are funded by our foundation partners, the most significant of which is the Andrew W. Mellon Foundation. We couldn't do what we do without these partners, who are remarkably capacious in their thinking and generous in their funding, and we've been very fortunate to have been able to develop such productive relationships with them.

In various interviews and in reading Michèle Lamont's book How Professors Think, **I've been surprised to see that literary scholars have generally received fewer fellowships than those in other fields, most**

notably history. As a literary scholar yourself, and the president of a major grant-making institution, is that something you can speak to?

This is something we have been talking about for quite a while because the number of proposals in literature that get funded is often not proportional to the number of applications. That is true in grant competitions of other organizations as well. And those that do get through are often ones that have a strong historical element, or speak in a discourse that is shared with people in historical fields, which is perhaps more immediately accessible. Several years ago, two eminent literary scholars on our board wondered about the relatively low success rate and actually took the time to read the rejected proposals. They ended up concurring with the panels' decisions.

It is somewhat confounding, but I can offer an explanation that is part data-driven and part anecdotal. The first stage of our screening process involves people reading proposals in their discipline, and the second stage is a review by an interdisciplinary panel. You have to get by the specialists first, and we have conducted statistical analyses that show that literary scholars are more severe in their evaluation of one another than is the case in some other fields. At the interdisciplinary panel level, it is my impression that literature proposals can founder, perhaps paradoxically, because their thrust is either too internal or too external. On the one hand, the use of some theoretical jargon can be opaque to a nonspecialist audience (and this is true of other fields as well). On the other, the increasingly historical or sociological claims of some literary projects do not pass muster in the eyes of specialists in those disciplines.

These challenges notwithstanding, a review of our roster of awards will show that many literature scholars succeed in our fellowship competitions.

Could you talk a little bit about the ACLS's evaluation process? How does it work?

The initial intake is done by staff here, who simply determine whether the applicant is eligible for the competition. Everything else is done by peer review in a two-step process, as I just mentioned. All the applications are read by three people in closely related fields, or as closely related as possible. You can imagine the volume of labor this involves. We have to get scads of reviewers. Each competition may have a thousand applicants, we need three readers for each of them, and [we] have to ask four people in order to get one. So our staff spends a lot of time getting people to do the first level of screening.

The three reviewers submit scores for proposals, and on that basis we form a short list for each panel to evaluate. We don't give any panel more than fifty applications to read, so there is a big cut at that point. Only about 30 percent of the application pool makes it to the final interdisciplinary panel review. Each selection committee consists of five people who come to our offices and spend an entire day (sometimes more) discussing the proposals. They have graded them in advance, but we always stress that those grades should not be considered dispositive. They are a starting point. We ask the panels to talk about each proposal, and they give them all a fair hearing. Very few sail through to an award.

I've been struck by testimony from many people on the degree of collegiality people find on these panels. How do you explain it, given the stakes and the opportunities for disagreement?

We try to pick people who will do a good job. We want people who are both broad-minded and tough-minded. The panels are diverse in geography, field, ethnicity, gender, institution, etcetera, but one universal characteristic we look for is whether a person is known to "play well with others." If panelists can't do that, they don't get invited back. When you do have someone who doesn't know how to be respectful and collegial, it makes for a long day. We've been very lucky in that that is very rare. I am always impressed at how smart our panels are, how thoroughly they have done their homework, how articulate they are. They're always very specific in both their criticism and praise. They are very willing to listen to one another and change their views through discussion with colleagues. The quality of the discussion is very high.

Are there any downsides to this very collegial, consensus-driven process? One person suggested to me that such systems are not the best at identifying truly innovative work.

That has not been my experience at ACLS. The projects we have funded run the gamut from traditional to innovative. There are two other things I would say. First, the panels are not permanent: members may be appointed for three years, but their terms are staggered, so there are new perspectives every year. Second, the people who serve on these panels tend to be very self-reflective and knowledgeable about higher education in general. They are aware of the trends in their fields, and they are attentive to what might be seen as overly conservative positions. I honestly don't think this is a case of a self-perpetuating elite. Generally, the panels all work very hard and well, and they always say it was worth it. They leave feeling very good about the work they have done. One case I remember was that of a very acerbic philosopher who came in with a good deal of skepticism about the process, and told me afterward that he felt much better about it after he had participated in it himself. He also felt much better about the state of the humanities in general.

One thing that often trips up younger scholars is the task of discussing other people's scholarship. What advice do you have for them?

This is not a problem that only younger people struggle with. Scholars of all ages do. Everyone has to be very careful to situate their work in the larger context of existing scholarship. Panelists notice if there is something that should be in the bibliography but isn't there. You have to make sure you have accounted for what has gone before, and to place yourself within an existing conversation.

Does theory present similar problems?

My sense is that if theory is integral to the framing of the applicant's topic, it tends not to be a problem. When it seems like theory is pasted-on after the fact, that is when you are going to have a hard time. Theory is what enables you to ask interesting questions. It should make sense in the context of your research. And, as I mentioned earlier, it's important to make sure that the theoretical language you use can be understood by a nonspecialist.

How should applicants choose their recommenders?

You should ask people who know you or know about you and your work. Getting a big name to write for you isn't going to help you if they can't speak to your work with specificity and detail. A really good letter is going to understand and explain both what the proposal is doing, and what the larger implications are for the field. Sometimes the recommendation explains the proposal better than the proposal itself does, and the letter writer can inadvertently make the proposal less competitive. The only thing applicants can do to prevent that is to get the proposal done early enough that colleagues and advisers can help iron out the kinks.

What other advice do you have for aspiring ACLS fellows?

Get started as early as you can. Often people wait for some chunk of free time to write their proposals that never comes. There is a strong correlation between the amount of time you spend on a proposal and the success rate. I've just mentioned the importance of getting advice from colleagues in your field. Once you have finished the proposal, get an academic in a different field to read it and comment on it. That is a good gauge of how successful you are in speaking to people in different disciplines. A further piece of advice is make sure it is a clean application. Proofread it. There is nothing more annoying than solecisms and misspellings. This may sound minor, but first impressions count. Finally, remember that the percentage of proposals that get accepted is terribly small. If you get rejected, don't hesitate to apply again. You can learn from failure. There is no black mark on you for having been unsuccessful in the past, as many applicants have discovered the second time around.

Notes

1. PREPARE FOR A COMPETITIVE PROCESS

1. Shira Boss, "The Greatest Mystery: Making a Best Seller," *New York Times*, May 13, 2007, www.nytimes.com/2007/05/13/business/yourmoney/13book. html (accessed January 19, 2018).

2. BE AMBITIOUS

1. Ramie Targoff, *Posthumous Love: Eros and the Afterlife in Renaissance England* (Chicago: University of Chicago Press, 2014).

3. ASSEMBLE A TEAM

1. Walt Whitman, *Leaves of Grass*, (New York: Modern Library, 1892), 392.
2. Annette Lareau, *Unequal Childhoods: Class, Race, and Family Life* (Berkeley: University of California Press, 2003).
3. Edward O. Wilson, *Letters to a Young Scientist* (New York: W.W. Norton, 2014), 144–147.
4. Adam Grant, *Give and Take: Why Helping Others Drives Our Success* (New York: Penguin, 2014).
5. William S. Burroughs, "Advice for Young People," https://www.youtube.com/watch?v=YqBIgCb7dv0 (accessed January 19, 2018).
6. Gavin De Becker, *The Gift of Fear, and Other Survival Signals That Protect Us from Violence* (New York: Random House, 1999).

4. CRAFT A COMPELLING QUESTION

1. Margaret Chowning, *Wealth and Power in Provincial Mexico: Michoacán from the Late Colony to the Revolution* (Stanford, CA: Stanford University Press, 1999), 8.
2. James Merrell, *Into the American Woods: Negotiations on the Pennsylvania Frontier* (New York: W.W. Norton, 2000); Nancy Farriss, *Maya Society under Colonial Rule: The Collective Enterprise of Survival* (Princeton, NJ: Princeton University Press, 1984).

5. BRAINSTORM WITHIN YOUR SUBJECT

1. D. A. Brading, *The First America: The Spanish Monarchy, Creole Patriots, and the Liberal State, 1492–1866* (Cambridge, UK: Cambridge University Press, 1993).
2. Edward O. Wilson, *Consilience: The Unity of Knowledge* (New York: Vintage, 1999), 59.
3. These references come from Richard Cobb, *The Police and the People: French Popular Protest, 1789–1820* (Oxford, UK: Oxford University Press, 1970), 264–266.

4. Janet Browne, *Charles Darwin: A Biography*, vol. 1: *Voyaging* (Princeton, NJ: Princeton University Press, 1996), 338.

5. When you put a single footnote marker at the end of the paragraph, you will simply separate each citation in the footnote with a semicolon, as I've done in this book with the endnotes.

6. DIVE INTO THE SCHOLARSHIP

1. Jonathan D. Spence, *The Search for Modern China*, 2nd ed. (New York: W.W. Norton, 1999), xx.

2. Ibid., xxi.

3. Quentin Skinner, "Duellist," in *New York Review of Books*, January 24, 1980, http://www.nybooks.com/articles/1980/01/24/duellist/ (accessed January 19, 2018).

7. KNOW YOUR THEORY

1. John Womack, "Doing Labor History: Feelings, Work, Material Power," in *Journal of the Historical Society* 5, no. 3 (September 2005): 278.

2. For a searching essay on the uses and limits of Foucault's ideas, see Laura Engelstein, "Combined Underdevelopment: Discipline and the Law in Imperial and Soviet Russia," in *American Historical Review* 98, no. 2 (April 1993): 338–353, and the responses to it that follow. To begin exploring Bourdieu's influence, see Jeffrey J. Sallaz and Jane Zavisca, "Bourdieu in American Sociology, 1980–2004," *Annual Review of Sociology* 33 (2007): 21–30, C1–C3, 31–41. On using Scott to interpret Austen, see Marcia McClintock Folsom, "Power in Mansfield Park: Austen's Study of Domination and Resistance," in *Persuasions: The Jane Austen Journal* 34 (2012).

3. Peter Burke, *History and Social Theory*, 2d ed. (Ithaca, NY: Cornell University Press, 2005).

4. Ibid., 18.

5. Michèle Lamont, *How Professors Think: Inside the Curious World of Academic Judgment* (Cambridge, MA: Harvard University Press, 2010), 18.

6. Lance R. Blyth, *Chiricahua and Janos: Communities of Violence in the Southwestern Borderlands, 1680–1880* (Lincoln: University of Nebraska Press, 2012), ix–x.

7. Robert Nozick, *The Examined Life: Philosophical Meditations* (New York: Simon & Schuster, 1989), 33.

11. GENERATE AN OUTLINE

1. Robert Nozick, *Philosophical Explanations* (Cambridge, MA: Harvard University Press, 2013), back cover copy.

2. Antonin Scalia and Brian Garner, *Making Your Case: The Art of Persuading Judges* (New York: Thomson West, 2008).

3. James Boswell, *The Life of Johnson* (New York: Penguin, 2008), 287.

12. CREATE A FIRST DRAFT

1. Susan Sheehan, *Is There No Place on Earth for Me?* (New York: Vintage, 1982), 3–4.
2. Ibid.
3. Moisés Naím, *Illicit: How Smugglers, Traffickers, and Copycats Are Hijacking the Global Economy* (New York: Random House, 2005), 1.
4. Brian DeLay, *War of a Thousand Deserts: Indian Raids and the U.S.-Mexican War* (New Haven: Yale University Press, 2008), xiii.
5. Louise Walker, *Waking from the Dream: Mexico's Middle Classes after 1968* (Stanford, CA: Stanford University Press, 2013), 16–17.
6. DeLay, *War*, xiv.
7. Neil Foley, *Quest for Equality: The Failed Promise of Black-Brown Solidarity* (Cambridge, MA: Harvard University Press, 2010), 1.
8. William Shakespeare, *Romeo and Juliet*, Folger Shakespeare Library (New York: Washington Square Press, 1992), 7.
9. Delay, *War*, xv.
10. Foley, *Quest*, 19.
11. Richard Marius, *Martin Luther: The Christian between God and Death* (Cambridge, MA: Harvard University Press, 2000), xiii.
12. J. Anthony Lukas, *Common Ground: A Turbulent Decade in the Lives of Three American Families* (New York: Vintage, 1986), 3.
13. Ibid., 651.
14. Janet Browne, *Charles Darwin: A Biography*, vol. 1: *Voyaging* (Princeton, NJ: Princeton University Press, 1996), 291.
15. Richard Marius, *A Writer's Companion*, 4th ed. (New York: McGraw Hill, 1998); on the prevalence of bad textbooks, see Marius, "Composition Studies," in Stephen Greenblatt and Giles Gunn, *Redrawing the Boundaries: The Transformation of English and American Literary Studies* (New York: Modern Language Association of America, 1992), 466–481.

14. JAMES F. BROOKS

1. James F. Brooks, *Captives and Cousins: Slavery, Kinship, and Community in the Southwest Borderlands* (Chapel Hill: University of North Carolina Press, 2002); James F. Brooks, ed., *Confounding the Color Line: The Indian-Black Experience in North America* (Lincoln: University of Nebraska Press, 2002); Mary Ann Irwin and James F. Brooks, eds., *Women and Gender in the American West* (Albuquerque: University of New Mexico Press, 2004); James F. Brooks, Christopher R. N. DeCorse, and John Walton, eds., *Small Worlds: Method, Meaning, and Narrative in Microhistory* (Santa Fe, NM: School for Advanced Research Press, 2008); Benedict J. Colombi and James F. Brooks, eds., *Keystone Nations: Indigenous Peoples and Salmon in the North Pacific* (Santa Fe, NM: School for Advanced Research Seminar Series, 2012); and James F. Brooks, *Mesa of Sorrows: A History of the Awat'ovi Massacre* (New York: W.W. Norton, 2016).

2. A description of the University of Iowa Mobile Museum can be found at http://discover.research.uiowa.edu/mobile-museum (accessed January 18, 2018).

3. Tiya Miles, *The House on Diamond Hill: A Cherokee Plantation Story* (Chapel Hill: University of North Carolina Press, 2010).

4. Charles Ragin and Howard Becker, *What Is a Case? Exploring the Foundations of Social Inquiry* (Cambridge, UK: Cambridge University Press, 1992).

5. Brooks, *Mesa of Sorrows*.

15. LIZABETH COHEN

1. Lizabeth Cohen, *Making a New Deal: Industrial Workers in Chicago, 1919–1939*, 2nd ed. (Cambridge, UK: Cambridge University Press, 2008); Lizabeth Cohen, *A Consumers' Republic: The Politics of Mass Consumption in Postwar America* (New York: Vintage, 2003); David Kennedy and Lizabeth Cohen, *The American Pageant* (Belmont, CA: Wadsworth, 2007).

2. Susan Rabiner and Alfred Fortunato, *Thinking Like Your Editor: How to Write Great Serious Nonfiction and Get It Published* (New York: W. W. Norton, 2002).

16. THOMAS B. F. CUMMINS

1. Thomas B. F. Cummins, *Huellas del Pasado: Los Sellos de Jama-Coaque Banco Central del Ecuador* (Quito: Museos del Banco Central del Ecuador, 1996); Thomas B. F. Cummins, *Toasts with the Inca: Andean Abstraction and Colonial Images on Kero Vessels* (Ann Arbor: University of Michigan Press, 2002); Elizabeth Hill Boone and Tom Cummins, eds., *Native Traditions in the Colonial World*, Dumbarton Oaks symposium volume, 1992, http://www.academia.edu/26660875/Elizabeth_Hill_Boone_and_Tom_Cummins_-_Native_traditions_in_the_postconquest_world (accessed February 3, 2018); Thomas B. F. Cummins and Betty Anderson, eds., *The Getty Murúa: Essays on the Making of Martín de Murúa's "Historia General del Piru"* (Los Angeles: J. Paul Getty Trust, 2008), http://www.getty.edu/publications/virtuallibrary/0892368945.html (accessed February 3, 2018).

17. ANTHONY GRAFTON

1. Anthony Grafton, *Defenders of the Text: The Traditions of Scholarship in an Age of Science, 1450–1800* (Cambridge, MA: Harvard University Press, 1991); Anthony Grafton, *Bring Out Your Dead: The Past as Revelation* (Cambridge, MA: Harvard University Press, 2001).

18. STEPHEN GREENBLATT

1. Stephen Greenblatt, *The Swerve: How the World Became Modern* (New York: W. W. Norton, 2012); Stephen Greenblatt, *Shakespeare's Freedom* (Chicago: University of Chicago Press, 2012); Stephen Greenblatt, *Will in the World: How Shakespeare Became Shakespeare* (New York: W. W. Norton, 2004); Stephen Greenblatt, *Hamlet in Purgatory* (Princeton, NJ: Princeton University Press, 2002); Stephen

Greenblatt, *Marvelous Possessions: The Wonder of the New World* (Chicago: University of Chicago Press, 1991); Stephen Greenblatt, *Renaissance Self-Fashioning: From More to Shakespeare* (Chicago: University of Chicago Press, 1983).

19. MICHÈLE LAMONT

1. Michèle Lamont, *Money, Morals, and Manners: The Culture of the French and the American Upper-Middle Class* (Chicago: University of Chicago Press, 1992); Michèle Lamont, *The Dignity of Working Men: Morality and the Boundaries of Race, Class, and Immigration* (Cambridge, MA: Harvard University Press, 2000); Michèle Lamont, *How Professors Think: Inside the Curious World of Academic Judgment* (Cambridge, MA: Harvard University Press, 2009).
2. Michèle Lamont and Laurent Thévenot, *Rethinking Comparative Cultural Sociology: Repertoires of Evaluation in France in the United States* (Cambridge, UK: Cambridge University Press, 2000); Peter A. Hall and Michèle Lamont, *Successful Societies: How Institutions and Culture Affect Health* (Cambridge, UK: Cambridge University Press, 2009); Peter A. Hall and Michèle Lamont, *Social Resilience in the Neoliberal Era* (Cambridge, UK: Cambridge University Press, 2013); Michèle Lamont and Patricia White, eds., *Workshop on Interdisciplinary Standards for Systematic Qualitative Research*, report of workshop held May 19–20, 2005, https://www.nsf.gov/sbe/ses/soc/ISSQR_workshop_rpt.pdf (accessed February 3, 2018).
3. Charles Camic and Neil Gross, "Contemporary Developments in Sociological Theory: Current Projects and Conditions of Possibility," *Annual Review of Sociology* 24 (1998): 453–476.
4. Michèle Lamont, Graziella Moraes Silva, Jessica Welburn, Joshua Guetzkow, Nissim Mizrachi, Hanna Herzog, and Elisa Reis, *Getting Respect: Dealing with Stigma and Discrimination in the United States, Brazil, and Israel* (Princeton, NJ: Princeton University Press, 2016).
5. James Mahoney and Kathleen Thelen, *Advances in Comparative-Historical Analysis* (Cambridge, UK: Cambridge University Press, 2015).
6. Gary King, Robert O. Keohane, and Sidney Verba, *Designing Social Inquiry* (Princeton, NJ: Princeton University Press, 1994); Michèle Lamont and Patricia White, "The Evaluation of Systematic Qualitative Research in the Social Sciences," National Science Foundation supported workshop, 2008, https://scholar.harvard.edu/files/lamont/files/issqr_workshop_rpt.pdf (accessed January 18, 2018).

20. MICHAEL C. MUNGER

1. You can read Munger's blog Kids Prefer Cheese at http://mungowitzend.blogspot.com; the Euvolutionary Exchange blog is at http://euvoluntaryexchange.blogspot.com (both accessed February 3, 2018).

21. SHERRY SMITH

1. Sherry Smith, *Hippies, Indians, and the Fight for Red Power* (Oxford, UK: Oxford University Press, 2012); Sherry Smith, *Reimagining Indians: Native Americans through*

Anglo Eyes, 1880–1940 (Oxford, UK: Oxford University Press, 2000); Sherry
Smith and Brian Frehner, eds., *Indians and Energy: Exploitation and Opportunity in the
American Southwest* (Santa Fe, NM: SAR Press, 2010); and Sherry Smith, ed., *The
Future of the Southern Plains* (Norman: University of Oklahoma Press, 2003).

22. PAULINE YU

1. Pauline Yu, "Your Alabaster in This Porcelain: Judith Gautier's *Le livre de jade*,"
PMLA 122, no. 2 (March 2007): 464–482.

Index

accountability of grant makers, 93–94
acknowledgments in scholarly
   publications, 18
ambition, 3, 13–17, 101, 109, 112, 143
American Academy in Rome, 17
American Council of Learned Societies
   (ACLS), 17, 104, 109, 132–133, 147, 148,
   153–158; advice to applicants for
   fellowships, 158; Burkhardt fellowships
   for younger faculty, 124, 154; Charles A.
   Ryskamp Research Fellowship, 1, 9–10;
   evaluation process, 155–156;
   internationally focused scholarship,
   support for, 154; partnering with other
   foundations, 154; Public Fellows
   program, 154
American Historical Association (AHA), 45,
   121
Andrew W. Mellon Foundation, 154
anthropology: ethnohistory encompassing,
   148; as field of study, 13; object of
   research, 40; questions answered by
   influential books in field of, 36–37;
   review committee composition at School
   of Advanced Research, 92
anti-humanism, ways to stop, 95
archives, 59, 95, 107–108
arrogance, 45–46, 49
art history, 40, 56, 109
audiences: for job applicant vs. grant
   applicant, 119–120; knowledge of,
   137–138; reaching broader audience,
   95–96, 100, 110, 111, 125–126, 148

Bacon, Francis, 52–53
Basso, Keith, 98

Becker, Howard: *What Is a Case?*, 97
behaviorism, 134, 144
Benchley, Robert, 4
bibliographies, 4, 50, 112, 157
Bill and Melinda Gates Foundation, 141
Blyth, Lance: *Chiricahua and Janos: Communities of
   Violence in the Southwestern Borderlands,
   1680–1880*, 55–56
book publication: vs. article or series of
   articles proposals, 143; finishing book
   already started or turning dissertation
   into book, 16, 102, 110, 142; proposal
   for, compared to grant proposal, 153;
   trade book vs. academic book, 94
Boswell, James: *Life of Johnson*, 69
Bourdieu, Pierre, 53–54, 115, 119, 132
Brading, D. A.: *The First America: The Spanish
   Monarchy, Creole Patriots, and the Liberal State,
   1492–1866*, 40–41
brainstorming, 39–44; getting out ideas
   without self-criticism, 69–71
Brooks, James F., interview with, 91–98
Browne, Janet: *Voyaging*, 43–44, 84
Burke, Peter: *History and Social Theory*, 52–53
Burkhardt Residential Fellowships for
   Recently Tenured Scholars, 124, 154
Burroughs, William S., 27
Butler, Jon, 14
Butler, Judith, 130

Calhoun, Dan, 93
Cañizares-Esguerra, Jorge, 29
Cannadine, David, 121
careers: continual state of flux in, 25.
   See also job applicants
Castro, Justin, 47

Center for Advanced Studies (Princeton), 109
Center for Advanced Studies in Visual Art, 109
Center for International and Area Studies at Yale University, 14
Chappell, David, 86
Charles A. Ryskamp Research Fellowship of the American Council of Learned Societies, 1, 9–10
Chicago Manual of Style, 50, 73
Chomsky, Noam, 53
Chowning, Margaret, 33
Clements Center for Southwest Studies (Southern Methodist University), 1, 147, 150
Cohen, Lizabeth, interview with, 99–105
collaboration, 25, 108, 129; collective problem solving, 54. *See also* team-building and team work
College Arts Association, 109
competition: in academia, 27, 139; among recommenders, 151; among scholars in same field, 53–54; children of wealthy parents, competitive edge of, 19; criticism from competitors, 10–11; disqualifying self, 120; likelihood of receiving grant, 1–2, 97–98, 102, 113, 121; at Radcliffe Institute, 105; School of Advanced Research process, 92; validation of winning in light of, 11–12, 108. *See also* job applicants for academic posts; rejection and failure
conclusion in first draft, 81–83
Conley, Tom, 29
coursework, describing in grant process, 21, 23, 40, 67
creativity, 68–71
credibility, 100, 103
criteria of evaluation, 3, 60–64, 113, 128–129, 131–132. *See also* Fulbright-Hays International Dissertation Research Fellowship
critical theory, 130

criticism: of other scholars and colleagues, 2, 29, 49–50, 56–57, 100, 125; responses to, 11, 27, 48–49, 128; in writing group workshop, 85, 86–88
Cummins, Thomas B. F.: *Beyond the Lettered City*, 108; interview with, 106–113

Dahl, Robert A.: *How Democratic Is the American Constitution?*, 36–37
David Rockefeller Center for Latin American Studies (Harvard), 109
Davulis, Laura, 11
de Becker, Gavin: *The Gift of Fear*, 28
DeLay, Brian: *War of a Thousand Deserts: Indian Raids and the U.S.-Mexican War*, 75–76, 78, 79
development office, role of, 141
disciplines: bias in fellowship awards, 115, 131, 138; criteria of evaluation and, 61; dominant paradigms within, 145; excellence, variance in standards of, 104, 133; final product varying among, 142; subject matter and, 40; theory across, 130; uniqueness vs. cross-disciplinary appeal, 4–5, 13. *See also* interdisciplinarity; *specific social science or humanities discipline*
dissertations: change from dissertation advisers to members of the field as recommenders, 93; committee members as ongoing mentors, 145; development or completion grants for, 81, 87, 136, 153; improving quality of writing during process of, 116; as incremental advance in knowledge, 143; job search and, 120; one-sentence description of topic, 93; serving as adviser or on committee for, 118; turning dissertation into book, 16, 102, 110, 142. *See also* Fulbright-Hays International Dissertation Research Fellowship
draft writing. *See* first draft
dual-career families, 133–134
Duke University, 141, 144
Dumbarton Oaks, 109

private vs. public institutions of higher
learning, 133
professional violence, 28–29
pronoia of givers, 26
Public Fellows program, 154
The Public Historian, 94
public vs. private institutions of higher
learning, 133

qualitative vs. quantitative research, 134
questions. *See* research questions

Rabiner, Susan: *Thinking Like Your Editor: How to
Write Great Serious Nonfiction and Get It
Published*, 100
Radcliffe Center for Advanced Studies, 109
Radcliffe Institute, 100, 103–105
Ragin, Charles: *What Is a Case?*, 97
Ranis, Gustav, 14
Rappaport, Joanne: *Beyond the Lettered City*,
107–108
rational choice, 134, 144, 145
reciprocity among peers, 25–29
recommenders: active in field vs. retired,
118; advice on engaging, 20–24,
103–104, 116–118; better explanation of
proposal from recommender than from
applicant, 150, 157–158; change from
academic advisers to members of the
field, 21–24, 103–104, 117; competition
among, 151; criteria of evaluation and,
63; late request for recommendations,
20; management of, 19–25, 103–104,
116–117; nature of relationship with, 3,
19–20, 112, 117, 150; negative letters,
118, 151; sample email to send to, 21, 23;
selection of, 24–25, 103, 117–118,
150–151, 157–158; writing quality of,
150–151
refereed articles, 122
rejection and failure, 10, 121, 126, 147;
coping with, 139–140, 150; learning
from feedback, 113, 129, 139–140, 150;

persistence and applying again, 10, 64,
158. *See also* competition
relevance, 69, 94, 110, 111
Renaissance poetry, grant proposal on, 16–17
replicability, 130
research, preliminary, 39–40, 44, 63, 107,
129
research questions, 33–38; bad questions,
38; brainstorming within your subject,
39–44; examples of, 34–37; in first draft,
78–79, 93; framing, 41–42, 97, 128; in
grant proposal process, 3; reasonable
amount of evidence relevant to, 42–43;
synoptic view of, 34
research topics. *See* subject matter
residential fellowships: Getty Research
Institute, 108. *See also* Radcliffe Institute
respectful views: toward predecessors and
colleagues, 20–22, 46, 57, 95–96; toward
recommenders, 104
review committees. *See* evaluation processes
Rindfleisch, Bryan, 87
Ritchie, Roy, 149
rival views, treatment of. *See* scholarship
Rolland, Modesto, 47
Ryskamp Research Fellowship. *See* American
Council of Learned Societies

Santander Visiting Fellowship at the David
Rockefeller Center for Latin American
Studies, Harvard, 1
Sarbanes-Oxley Act (2002) and nonprofits,
93–94
Scalia, Antonin: *Making Your Case: The Art of
Persuading Judges*, 68–70
scholarship, 3, 45–50; accessibility of, 95,
97–98, 110, 155; building on prior
scholarship, 143, 157; in first drafts,
75–78; future of, 94; gap filling in field,
46–47, 75–78, 95, 147, 153; influential
books in fields of anthropology and
political science, 36–37; putdowns of
other scholars, 29, 49–50, 56–57, 100,